Policing and the Media

Policing and the Media
Facts, fictions and factions

**Frank Leishman and
Paul Mason**

WILLAN
PUBLISHING

Published by

Willan Publishing
Culmcott House
Mill Street, Uffculme
Cullompton, Devon
EX15 3AT, UK
Tel: +44(0)1884 840337
Fax: +44(0)1884 840251
e-mail: info@willanpublishing.co.uk
website: www.willanpublishing.co.uk

Published simultaneously in the USA and Canada by

Willan Publishing
c/o ISBS, 5824 N.E. Hassalo St,
Portland, Oregon 97213-3644, USA
Tel: +001(0)503 287 3093
Fax: +001(0)503 280 8832
e-mail: info@isbs.com
website: www.isbs.com

First published 2003

ISBN 1-903240-28-X Paperback
ISBN 1-903240-29-8 Hardback

British Library Cataloguing-in-Publication Data

A catalogue record for this book is available from the British Library

Project management by Deer Park Productions, Tavistock, Devon
Printed and bound by T.J. International Ltd, Padstow, Cornwall PL28 8RW

Contents

Acknowledgements

We have been inspired as individuals throughout our academic engagement with policing and the media by a number of colleagues, whose encouragement and friendship over many years is warmly acknowledged, particularly John Alderson, Martin Barker and Tom Wood. Both of us owe a huge intellectual debt to Professor Robert Reiner, in the shadow of whose scholarship so much of this book has been written. For moral support, perspective and many helpful comments along the way, we thank Chris Aldous, Nigel Brearley, Les Johnston, Lou Johnston and also Brian Willan for his trust in us to deliver and for his inestimable patience while he waited for that to happen. Especial thanks to Ange and Beth Leishman for their love and understanding and for tolerating far too many lost weekends during the course of this project. Paul thanks his parents, Larraine and John Mason, for all their love and support. All shortcomings remain ours.

Chapter 1

Introduction: reality, realism and representation

Reality, realism and representation

In introducing a special media-focused issue of the often under-celebrated *Criminal Justice Matters*, Kevin Stenson and Hazel Croall observed in their editorial:

> The media are not simply neutral conduits of information about crime; indeed, the institutional arrangements that organise the media and the rhetorical forms through which crime is represented can play a vital role in shaping and reflecting our deepest personal and cultural fears about crime and insecurity. (Stenson and Croall, 2001: 3)

We could equally substitute 'the police' for 'the media' in that quotation, which makes it, in our estimation, a useful thought to keep in mind throughout the ensuing chapters.

We have divided the book into three themed sections: facts, fictions and factions, though as will quickly become evident, the lines between such clear divisions are increasingly blurred and the concepts of reality, realism and representation slippery and complex.

Our first section focuses on the 'factual' and considers various dimensions of the construction, contents and effects of media images of policing and crime. In Chapter 2 we outline what is 'known' from previous studies and syntheses about the nature of crime coverage and its consequences in terms of possible effects on behaviour and in relation to the shaping of public perceptions of police efficiency and effectiveness.

Chapter 3 extends the discussion by exploring the dynamics of what R. C. Mawby (2002) calls 'police image work', an area of activity that has become increasingly professionalised in recent years. Using the media to promote themselves is a well established feature of American law enforcement organisations, the *FBI Law Enforcement Bulletin*, for example, frequently featuring articles with titles like 'Media interviews: a systematic approach for success' (Vance, 1997) and 'Fine tune your news briefing' (Sparks and Staszak, 2000). We note in Chapter 3 how the cause of corporate communications has been taken up enthusiastically by the British police (Boyle, 1999a), to the extent that media relations can no longer be regarded as a mere adjunct to police operations and strategic planning.

The three chapters in our 'fiction' section focus primarily on British televisual fictional representations of policing, a rich vein of the policing image on the small screen which has not been replicated in cinematic representations. Whereas one can reel off a string of memorable gangster movie titles such as, *Scarface* (1932), *White Heat* (1949) and *The Godfather* (1972), courtroom dramas such as *Twelve Angry Men* (1957) and *Jagged Edge* (1985) and prison films such as *Birdman of Alcatraz* (1962), *Midnight Express* (1978) and *The Shawshank Redemption* (1995), it is a much harder task to find equivalent police films – *Assault on Precinct 13* (1978), *Blue Steel* (1990) and *ID* (1995) perhaps. Reiner points out that 'Cop movies do not form a comparable generic pattern. At most, there has been a handful of relatively short cycles of movies about cops' (Reiner, 1981: 194–5).

While a genre of police films may be problematic in the cinema, it is possible to delineate a body of television drama whose focus is law enforcement and it is this which forms the content of Chapters 4, 5 and 6. Notions of 'a heritage of realism' and expansive iconography in these programmes complicate considerations of 'reality' and 'realism' in representations of policing and policework. Reiner (1994) comments that despite the prevalence of crime fiction dating back to the 1820s, the emergence of the police officer as protagonist is relatively recent. Even when they did finally appear, police figures were peripheral, playing second fiddle to heroic sleuths like Sherlock Holmes. It was not until the late 1940s that the police procedural appeared: 'mystery plots in which the investigation is undertaken by a professional police detective, portrayed as functioning as one of a team, not as an exceptionally gifted individual' (Reiner, 1994: 17). As we discuss in Chapter 4, the police procedural has been the focus of some of the most successful dramas in television history: *Dixon of Dock Green* ran for 18 years; *Z Cars*, which ran for 16 years, had audience ratings of 14 million during its first series

(Hurd, 1981); and *The Bill* which has been running for 18 years still reaches more than 10 million viewers a week.

The relationship between the reality of policing and these popular representations of it is complex, as Dyer describes:

> Reality is always more extensive and complicated than any system of representation can possibly comprehend and we always sense that this is so – representation never 'gets' reality which is why human history has produced so many different and changing ways of trying to get it. (Dyer, 1993: 3)

Representations of policing are relative to the individuals producing and consuming them. There is no neutral, objective representation of the police in fiction, hence notions of 'reality' and 'authenticity' are relative, although, as O'Shaughnessy observes, 'We may decide that one set of representations are true or that they are more true than others' (O'Shaughnessy, 1999: 40). Any assessment of the realism and authenticity of fictional representations of the police is based on the viewer's own knowledge and experience of them. Although this knowledge may have been acquired through some direct contact with the police, it is likely to be heavily supplemented with information gleaned from newspapers, television, radio, film and the Internet. Fictional portrayals, one such source, can be seen to address the gaps in viewer knowledge. This 'completion of the half-formed picture' (Hurd, 1981: 57) suggests that audiences tend to accept as true those parts of a drama that are beyond their experience. In research on *The Bill*, Mason (1992) notes how the clear-up rate for notifiable offences in 1990 was 34 per cent compared to 78.7 per cent in *The Bill*. Furthermore, audiences steeped in cop show tradition mean the police drama must incorporate a 'heritage of realism' from previous police shows. In Chapters 4 and 5 we show, for example, how the values first espoused in *Dixon of Dock Green* are still recognisable in police dramas of the twenty-first century.

While all cop shows are, to some extent, lineal descendants of George Dixon, the modern crime drama features police officers who are often less than a chip off the old cop and more splintered with rougher, less well-defined edges (Reiner, 2000a). In Chapter 6 we suggest that a thinner blurred line now exists between crime and law enforcement, where representations of the police are more complex and where rule-breaking is often an essential part of thief-taking. With moral uncertainty roaming the new 'copland', audiences seeking the comfortable and monochromatic world of good versus evil once inhabited by George Dixon must now turn to the synoptic realms of infotainment.

Chapters 7 and 8 examine various aspects of the uneasy amalgam of 'fact' and 'fiction' that often goes under the name of 'infotainment' or 'faction', the staple of which is the 'reality' TV cop show, such as *Blues and Twos* and *Police Camera Action*. The rise and popularity of this 'hybrid' form raises further uncomfortable questions about the interrelationships between reality, realism and representation. As Annette Hill notes:

> For many critics of reality programming, its sensational format has blurred the boundaries between information and entertainment to such an extent that it can no longer be associated with the aims of the traditional documentary. (2000: 232)

In Chapter 8, we discuss this underlying concern by speculating on the possible effects for policing and the justice process should the incursion of cameras into courtrooms be extended. It may seem a little far-fetched but the prospect of watching the activities of inmates of the 'Big Brother Court House' is, perhaps, the reality TV show concept that could truly 'end 'em all'.

Our primary purpose in writing this book has always been to produce a volume that brings together, in one place, a contemporary examination of the British policing image in all three domains of fact, fiction and faction. We hope, too, that it will inform and perhaps even entertain along the way.

Part One
Facts

Chapter 2

Contents and effects

Introduction

The police are paid to be suspicious and there can be little doubt that, as an occupational group, they tend to mistrust the media, with its agenda to entertain and propensity to misinform the public. However, if asked on some professional management development programme to conduct a SWOT (strengths–weaknesses–opportunities–threats) analysis around the theme of the media and its implications for policing, senior police officers would not find it difficult to contribute something to each quadrant, for example:

- strength – in that harnessing the media effectively to promote the police can in all likelihood do more to provide symbolic reassurance to more of the public for more of the time and at less cost than can a plethora of patrolling police officers;

- weakness – as in stumbling spokespersons and maladroit media management can have deleterious effects on public perceptions of the police and levels of confidence in them;

- opportunity – to present the organisation, its operations and its objectives (and of course oneself and one's own career ambitions) in a positive light;

- threat – because of the media's watchdog role and potential to expose areas of organisational ineffectiveness or malpractice.

Feeding into such an analysis would be a mix of professional experience, instinct, knowledge and, quite probably, prejudice about the contents and consequences of mass media coverage of crime and policing. This chapter offers a review of what is known from previous research and syntheses about these relationships and interrelationships, focusing around a cluster of questions which continue to preoccupy academics and practitioners alike, questions such as:

- What is the nature of the media's treatment of crime?

- On balance does this coverage present the police in a positive or negative light?

- Do media images cause crime?

- To what extent does media coverage promote fear of crime?

The first section addresses the first and second questions by reviewing conclusions from previous studies, while the second considers the 'effects' questions, around which a veritable research industry has arisen, especially with regard to violent images and their potential effects on children. Our focus in this chapter is primarily on the 'factual' media, though as will already be evident from the introduction, there is much crossover and boundary blurring at work, which serves to further complicate the media–policing equation, making it difficult to isolate completely the factual from the fictional and factional. As Howitt observes:

> Factual crime in newspapers and on radio and television is the result of a value-ridden news selection process. Partly the emphasis of news on drama which sensationalizes and personalizes events determines what is included. Nevertheless, what is read, heard and seen as news is something other than 'just the facts' … There is some reason to believe that much non-fictional coverage of crime shares some of the production values of fictional programmes. (1998: 28)

With that in mind let us identify some of the key issues.

Contents

As Robert Reiner has rightly noted (1997, 2000a, 2000b), throughout the twentieth century, public images of crime and policing have largely been constructed and contested via the various mass media which interact with audiences in a dialectical way, creating 'a complex loop of inter-dependence' (2000b: 53). This widening gyre generates recurring rafts of anxieties and questions about media contents and effects, resulting in debates which seem to have been revisited and intensified with each new development in communications technology from the humble transistor radio to high-tech text messaging WAPs (web access phones). The police themselves have often been prominent and vocal in articulating 'respectable fears' (Pearson, 1983) about the media's pernicious effects on morality. As Reiner recounts (1997), during the First World War, the Chief Constable of Wigan blamed the cinema for rises in juvenile crime, while some six decades later, James Anderton, Chief Constable of Greater Manchester, became associated with the late Mary Whitehouse's long-running campaign to clean up television. More recently, senior officers in London have publicly berated British movies like *Lock, Stock and Two Smoking Barrels* and certain advertisements for glamourising gun violence and 'laddish culture' (Fogg, 2000).

The characterisation of the media as criminogenic in the sense that they undermine respect for authority and catalyse 'copycatting' criminal behaviour, particularly amongst the young, has enjoyed more repeats over the years than the typical TV summer schedule. The thrust of this perspective was succinctly captured in the comment column of the middle-market tabloid *Daily Mail*. Reacting to a Broadcasting Standards Commission report which raised concerns about storylines in television 'soap' drama, the paper opined under the sub-head 'sordid soaps':

> Heroin addiction, domestic violence, prostitution, murder – all are routinely shown at times when, as programme-makers know perfectly well, children are certain to be watching. And nobody at the BBC or ITV seems unduly concerned at the coarsening effect all of this may have on impressionable young minds. (*Daily Mail*, 10 May 2002: 12)

This 'subversive' view of the media (Reiner, 1997) competes with an academically influential critical perspective that puts the media and the police in the dock for essentially colluding in creating crime waves and propagating the panics that fuel the public's respectable fears about the nature and risk of criminal victimisation. What Reiner dubs the 'hegemonic' view of media-made criminality is scathing of the media's heavy reliance on the police as 'primary definers' in the construction of news (Welch *et al.*, 1997). The mass mediated 'folk devil' has come in a variety of guises in the history of 'respectable fears', from Pearson's (1983) hooligans, through Cohen's (1972) mods and rockers, Hall *et al.*'s (1978) black muggers and, more recently, asylum seekers (Howard, 2001). As Hunt (1997) puts it, 'every moral panic has its scapegoat' and 'elite-engineered' crises of hegemony recurrently reinforce and perpetuate via the media myths about youth, race, ethnicity and crime (Hall *et al.*, 1978; Webster, 2001; see also Chapter 3). The resultant distorted picture of the 'crime problem' in the media ensures that the crimes of the powerful are rarely exposed and accounts, at least in part, for why these 'real villains' seldom have their white collars felt, while other sections of the community are routinely 'over-policed' (White and Perrone, 1997). In its extremest form, the 'media-as-hegemonic' thesis (Reiner, 1997: 190) demonises the media for demonising. Nevertheless, from this critical tradition have emerged compelling questions about the media and the nature of their relationship with the police as news sources, concerns that continue to have powerful resonance today.

Indecent exposure?

A recurrent finding from content analysis studies is that crime is an 'over-exposed' topic in the media generally, receiving a disproportionate amount of coverage relative to other major social issues, including what many would regard to be greater social harms. Estimates about the proportion of news output given over to crime show considerable variation, with some researchers (Reiner, 1997) placing it at well over half, depending upon the definitions and methodology used. What is not in dispute, however, are the facts that crime news is a global media staple and that reporting trends across continents show remarkable similarities (Reiner, 1997; Howitt, 1998).

Reiner, Livingstone and Allen, in their major study of mass media representations of crime and criminal justice since 1945, revealed a threefold increase in newspaper coverage of 'central crime' stories from between 7 and 9 per cent in the period 1945–51, to around 21 per cent between 1985 amd 1991 (Reiner *et al.*, 2000a: 182). A similar rising trend (albeit with some cyclical fluctuations in between) was discerned for stories on the criminal justice system and on crime policy. The proportion of media content given over to crime has typically been seen as linked to market position, with 'lower-market' tabloid newspapers such as *The Sun* exhibiting the highest proportion (Roshier, 1973; Williams and Dickinson, 1993). Reiner and his colleagues present persuasive evidence supporting a shift over the postwar period towards 'tabloidisation' of the quality press in matters of crime reporting, a finding that mirrors experience in the United States (Stepp, 1998). However, Reiner is correct to caution that, while the results of more recent content analysis studies would appear to suggest an increase of crime stories over earlier ones, 'it is not possible to conclude from a literature review whether there is a trend for a greater proportion of news to be about crime' (1997: 198).

It is well documented that the media tend to centre on the more serious offences (homicide, armed robbery and sexual assault) and this aspect of selectivity has been the focus of a number of studies of mass media treatment of crime (Reiner, 1997; Howitt, 1998). Much has been made in these of the disproportionate relationship between crimes of inter-personal violence as a percentage of total crime news output, compared with the 'corresponding' percentage of violent offences in the recorded crime statistics. A well-known analysis of Scottish newspaper reports by Ditton and Duffy (1983), for example, revealed that whereas violent and sexual crime accounted for less than 3 per cent of recorded crime, it occupied just under half of all crime news. Soothill and Walby (1991) identified an increasing 'over-representation' of sex crime in the news, with the proportion of rape cases being reported on rising from just under a quarter in 1951 to over a third in 1985. Williams and Dickinson's (1993) study revealed that, on average, almost two-thirds of newspaper space occupied by crime stories was taken up by items related to crimes of personal violence, compared with official estimates that such crimes account for around 6 per cent of crime overall. The same study found that, on average, one-eighth of 'event-oriented' news in the period analysed was about crime. Interestingly, an opinion poll conducted by the BBC suggested 'over-representation' of a similar magnitude in the minds of the audience, with its finding that, on average, people thought that more than a quarter of the population had been victims of violent crime that year, compared to less than 2 per cent in the official statistics (*The Guardian*, 3 January 1995). By contrast, acquisitive crimes that are statisti-cally more likely to occur (and, incidentally, less likely to be cleared up) such as theft, car crime and burglary are typically under-represented in crime news (Howitt, 1998). Reporting on interim findings from an unpublished audit of crime news coverage in television, radio and newspapers, Howitt and colleagues found that for all media combined, whereas 68 per cent of stories related to crimes against the person, only 9 per cent concerned property crime (Howitt, 1998: 35). Similar patterns have been uncovered for other jurisdictions (Reiner, 1997): paradoxically, the crimes that media consumers are themselves most likely to have direct experience of are less likely to receive high-profile media attention.

There is a tendency for the media to focus on solved crimes, typically through coverage of arrest and trial outcomes, with courtroom reporting traditionally emphasising the prosecution case and the judge's summing-up (Reiner, 2000b: 141). These days, however, crime reporting seems increasingly to accentuate a 'cop-sided' view (Reiner, 2000), with pre-trial investigative developments being disseminated via police press release and set-piece press conference, and reactions to trial outcomes more often than not articulated in broadcast news by investigating officers issuing soundbites to camera on the crown court steps (see also Chapter 8). While criminologists are acutely aware of the phenomenon of the attrition rate, which reveals that fewer than 5 per cent of all offences committed are cleared up, and only around 2 per cent actually end up in a conviction (Croall, 1998: 22), media coverage can thus serve to induce in the public mind, an inflated impression of both crime solvability and police prowess in detection. The more solvable crimes are precisely the sort of crimes already mentioned, homicide and sexual offences, not simply because of their seriousness, 'political resonance' (Howitt, 1998) and the additional resources that the police might make available for such investigations, but also more mundanely because these tend to be 'self-solving' (Innes, 1999), not least because the perpetrator and victim have usually had some prior association with one another. Perceptions of police skill and efficiency are thus bolstered and boosted by the reinforcement of success in the serious and sensational crime categories, which predictably can have both negative and positive consequences for the police organisation. On the one hand, the public may be reassured that the police are effective at catching criminals, yet on the other, this over-inflation of the police's efficacy can come back to haunt them when they fail, as frequently they do, to match the public's media-fuelled and, in many senses, unrealistic expectations of their crime-busting capabilities.

The case of drugs and drug-related crime – another overexposed topic in the news – is a good example of how media opportunity and PR strength can convert over time to threat or weakness. During the 1980s, the police were very much in the vanguard of the 'war against drugs'; however, as Karim Murji has suggested:

> Following their role in the spectacular representation of drugs as a problem and continuing evidence that usage has not declined, the police are faced with two possibilities: either to 'give up' and join the drug legalisation lobby, or to campaign for even more powers and resources, etc. Both options position them in a posture of defeat: the 'problem' is either insoluble, or so overwhelming that only further special powers, the limits of which can never be specified, will do. (Murji, 1998: 131)

Howitt (1998: 167) makes the pertinent observation with regard to drugs that the police, in part because of their social isolation, may have been particularly susceptible to 'acting up' to media stereotypes of drug-users. This can lead to heightened police attempts to contain and control the 'problem' with consequent 'spiralling' effects in the mass-mediated image of drug-use and social reaction to this. Police target those identified as the 'problem population', processing more suspects, generating 'rises' in drug statistics leading to increased concern about the extent of the problem and escalating demands that the police get even tougher with those labelled as 'druggies': in other words 'deviancy amplification' in action (Young, 1971).

Offensive profiling?

The media distorts the profile of victims as well as that of typical offenders, as is summarised by Reiner (1997, 2000a, 2000b), who notes that the demography of the media-constructed villain and victim (in fiction as well as 'fact') tends to be skewed towards the older, white, middle- or upper-class individual, in contrast to the picture that emerges from official crime statistics and victimisation surveys. While the media may promote 'moral panics' that scapegoat youth as offensive and offending, they tend to focus less on young people (except, of course, the very young) as victims, although again successive sweeps of the British Crime Survey (BCS) indicate that the young, especially young men, are more likely to be the victims of crimes of interpersonal violence. Stanko encapsulates the 'composite picture' of the victim that has emerged from crime survey findings: 'he is young, single, unemployed, socially active outside the home, probably drinks and shares many characteristics with the young man who is his assailant' (2000: 18). Contrary to media stereotypes, victims of street muggings are typically not the vulnerable old lady having her handbag snatched, but the teenager being relieved by a coeval of a mobile phone (Harrington and Mayhew, 2001).

Whereas crime is known to be unevenly distributed throughout the population, tending to be concentrated in the most deprived urban neighbourhoods (Croall, 1998), the media focus is usually on the mature, more affluent, 'respectable' victim. There may also be, as journalist Jonathan Duffy (2002) has suggested, a disproportionate national media focus on crimes committed in London, though that probably does not extend to the City of London. As in criminology, so in the media's and in the police's own institutional priorities, white-collar crime, its perpetrators and its victims are generally conspicuous by their absence, despite the widespread acknowledgement of a huge unreported figure of such offences. While high-profile cases like Robert Maxwell's pension fund fleecing and the more recent Jonathan Aitken and Jeffrey Archer perjury convictions have been given the 'folk devil' treatment (Levi, 2001) more usually reserved for 'hot-spot' hooligans and lager louts, in general media coverage concentrates on street crimes that stimulate the *fears* of the respectable, while simultaneously sidelining the *crimes* of the respectable (Tombs and Whyte, 2001; Slapper and Tombs, 1999).

In both crime news and crime statistics, offending is predominantly a male activity (Sacco, 1995), though, from time to time, the media stands indicted for 'misquoting' research on 'girl violence' and spreading myths about violent behaviour among young women (Batchelor, 2001). The issue of race and crime, as mentioned earlier, is recurrently controversial but, as Reiner (1997: 201) evaluates, evidence of over-representation of members of the ethnic minorities as lawbreakers in newspaper reports has been contradictory. However, a recent American content analysis of local TV news coverage by Dixon and Linz (2000) revealed that blacks and Latinos were significantly more likely than whites to be represented as lawbreakers, with blacks being disproportionately represented in comparison to official crime rates. In the same study, whites were found to be under-represented as lawbreakers, but over-represented as law defenders. Interestingly, while blacks were neither over- nor under-represented as police officers, Latinos were under-represented when compared to corresponding employment records. Replication in Britain of this kind of study, which attempts to combine inter-group, inter-role and inter-reality comparisons with insights into the likely psychological impact of such images, might be worthwhile at a time when police forces are endeavouring to meet challenging Home Office targets to boost recruitment and retention of ethnic minority officers.

As Stanko (2000: 25) discusses, a perennial theme in victimology concerns the dualism of 'blameworthy' and 'blameless' victim status. Reporting of rape and other sex crime cases is an area where the attachment of 'blame' or otherwise to individual victims is neither uncommon nor uncontroversial (Lees, 1995). When the police themselves are victims of a crime, media reactions to this can also be contradictory. The murder of a British police officer on duty, for example WPC Yvonne Fletcher killed during the Libyan Embassy siege in London in 1984, is thankfully statistically rare. Yet it remains one of the most potent and culturally salient symbols of threat to the established social order. The same sense of shock also applies to the murder of popular fictional police officers, PC George Dixon's demise in the *The Blue Lamp* being the classic example (see Chapter 4). The killing of a police officer unfailingly attracts cross-media outrage and sympathy, generally eliciting calls from leader writers, police leaders and leading politicians for tougher sentencing and penalties, including the reintroduction of capital punishment. However, the intensity of the media treatment of the horrific hacking to death of PC Keith Blakelock during the 1986 Broadwater Farm riots, and in particular the demonisation of Winston Silcott, was directly implicated in the Tottenham 3 miscarriage of justice scandal (Reiner, 2000b: 207). In riot and public order situations when police officers (and police dogs and police horses, for that matter) are on the receiving end of physical violence, photographs of bloodied casualties from the scene regularly make the front pages, the unfortunate injured officers and animals tending to be associated with a collective 'us' as opposed to 'them' out there who perpetrated the act. However, interestingly, as reaction to recent damages claims brought by serving police officers for incidences of post-traumatic stress disorder might suggest, neither the media nor the public seem to regard the police unconditionally as 'blameless' victims of criminal injuries (BBC Online, 2 March 2001).

It can be claimed that the way in which the media tend to portray the police is very much in the 'crime-fighter' mould, characterising them as the 'thin blue line', a kind of *cordon sanitaire* against advancing tides of lawlessness, providing a reassuring, risk-reducing presence on the streets, screens and, increasingly, in cyberspace too (Wall, 2001). The recurrent use of martial and disease metaphors – words such as war, battle, and invasion; epidemic, cancer and sickness – in connection with issues such as drugs, public disorder and asylum seekers underlines this very strongly, bestowing a kind of collective heroic status on the police organisation, which is typically referred to as 'overstretched' in contrast to 'inadequate' parents, 'inexperienced' social workers and 'permissive' prison governors (Sparks, 2001b). As Fowler notes, such 'terms of abuse and endearment' reflect the media's preoccupation 'with sorting people into categories and placing discriminatory values upon them' (1991: 110). Even if intended as what Sparks refers to as an 'allocation of censure', ' "overstretched" police force' is an appellation which connotes a valiant few, bravely struggling against a superior enemy. It conjures up an image of *300 Spartans* in *Fort Apache the Bronx*: strength in weakness – in those famous words of Sir Robert Mark, 'winning by appearing to lose' (see Chapter 3).

It is perhaps worthy of mention here that the overwhelming focus in the media is on the 'public' police, despite the evident plurality and diversity that makes up policing in late modernity (Johnston, 2000). Mark Button (2002) provides a helpful taxonomy of this diversity, which updates and extends Johnston's earlier (1992) work. Button's classification of 'hybrid policing' embraces an expansive assemblage of central and decentralised bodies, specialised police organisations and non-private security and private policing bodies. Under the subcategory of 'voluntary policing', Button also mentions the investigative activities of the media themselves, epitomised in programmes such as *The Cook Report, World in Action* and, more recently, *MacIntyre Undercover*. However, in the rolling script of the event-oriented crime news story, it is the public police who are still essentially presented as the solvers and solution to the 'crime problem', an impression of the police that, as we shall see, is constantly reinforced by fictional representations (see Chapters 4 and 5) and the myriad hybrid categories of 'infotainment' (Chapter 7).

Performance under pressure

When police officers misbehave, there has historically been a tendency for the media to recast the police institution in a favourable light – the 'one bad apple in the otherwise clean barrel' narrative, which serves simultaneously to question and reproach, yet in the end restore police legitimacy (Reiner, 2000b: 142). This appears to be linked inextricably to the working ideology of news reporters, who see themselves as having a fundamental moral duty to support 'goodies' over 'baddies'. This is a recurring theme among crime reporters interviewed by Chibnall (1977) and Schlesinger and Tumber (1994), whose accounts reveal a pronounced sense that responsible journalism implies support for the police, albeit 'suspicious support'. In the words of one correspondent interviewed by Chibnall (1977: 143):

> If you always accept that the police are right that is dangerous and can encourage abuses [but on the other hand] what you don't want to do is make the police's job harder – you want to make it easier because that is the way to improve society as a whole. Newspapers are firmly on the side of law and order, you've got to have that or society would collapse.

From our own experience as lecturers, this sentiment – perhaps not unsurprisingly – accords with the views expressed by journalism students also.

However, in line with Reiner's (1998) bifurcation thesis, which suggests that the moral status and probity of the police are now constantly under scrutiny, the 'one bad apple' formula has become ever harder to sustain, as media reaction to more recent scandals such as the Stephen Lawrence Inquiry and the Damilola Taylor trial have demonstrated. In this post-critical era, argues Reiner, an increasing minority of crime stories do now routinely portray police as 'either irrelevant, ineffective or deviant', thus:

> The performance of policing is tested pragmatically for its value to individual clients, as much in media representations, as in the practice of policing in the age of the Audit Commission. (1998: 28)

This is a theme that we return to in Chapter 6.

Since the 1980s, the police have become ever more driven by the three 'E's of economy, effectiveness and efficiency introduced in the seminal Home Office Circular 114/83 (Leishman and Savage, 1993) which sought to extend to policing the concept of Value for Money (VFM) which had previously been promoted in other areas of the public sector. This set of imperatives has been intensified in recent years across the public sector by the Best Value regime and the influence of the Audit Commission (Butler, 2000) and, in this environment, pressure on policing resources combined with pressure to achieve an astonishing array of performance targets have placed additional importance on the role of the media as both an opportunity and a resource in many areas of policing activity (see also Chapter 3). But as the media coverage of drugs has highlighted, when police strategies are linked to high-profile 'zero tolerance' campaigns, engaging the media can draw the police into a threatening spider's web of three alternative 'E's – *exhortation* (to pursue tough tactics), *expectation* (that these will achieve results) and, ultimately, *excoriation* (when 'the wheel comes off' and ineffective and/or corrupt practices float to the surface). Nonetheless, despite the view deeply held by many police that they are the repeat victims of mass media malevolence and manipulation, the broad thrust of news coverage of crime and policing does appear ultimately to be supportive of the police as an institution and to depict them as successful and dynamic crime-fighters. As Richard Sparks suggests, crime news stories 'impose moral structure and intelligibility on the swirling chaos of events' (2001b: 6). In the process of so doing, the factual media represent the police as struggling bravely against the odds, thus reaffirming traditional 'common-sense' approaches to law and order, even if trust and belief in them is less unquestioning that it once may have been.

Effects

If police chiefs may gather some comfort that media messages about policing are generally supportive of the institution and are thus potentially a useful ally in seeking to secure political support as well as more resources from the Home Office, they will still harbour misgivings about the potential negative effects of the media. They will be concerned, for instance, at the extent to which the over-exposure of serious crime in media reports will impact on levels of public anxiety about personal and community safety, and the consequent demands and expectations for service that this may present for their forces. As we have suggested, several senior police spokespersons have, over the years, sided with Reiner's (1997) 'media-as-subversive' perspective, which views the media as a threat to public order and morals. As we shall see in Chapter 8, chief constables have also been prominent critics of the role that the media plays in undermining due process of justice, through practices such as 'chequebook journalism'. As Cashmore (1994: ch. 5) observes, media effects debates revolve around two principal axes: firstly the notion that deviance on the media causes deviant behaviour in society; and second, that fear of crime is cultivated by excessive consumption of crime coverage in the media. Let us consider each in turn.

Ill or nil effects?

As already mentioned, the arrival of each new mass media development, from bawdy burlesque to broadband broadcasting, has been accompanied by concerns about its potential criminogenic effects. In much the way that witchcraft was implicated in criminal activities in the Dark and Middle Ages, the effects of the media have been the butt of blame in late modernity. Shocking cases such as the murder of James Bulger have prompted speculation of a connection with violent videos (Barker, 1997), while the proximity of the mass gun attacks in Dunblane and Port Arthur (Howitt, 1998: 77) raised troubling questions about potential copycat effects. More recently, the music of Marilyn Manson was floated as one possible explanation for the horrific 'trenchcoat mafia' shootings at Columbine High School in Colorado (Barker and Petley, 2001). In the aftermath of such appalling and exceptional events, campaigners have been quick to seize upon research findings that appear to support causal links between criminal behaviour and media effects. As Barker and Petley observe:

> ... moral campaigners love a nice-looking statistic, even if that statistic is meaningless or unreliable (and of course the most meaningless of all is the assumption that 'violence' is an abstractable unit whose presence can be counted and whose 'influence' can be studied). (2001: 3)

More recent effects studies have picked up on the fact that viewers make distinctions between incidents of 'violence' depending on the context within which they occur. Viewers' sense of justice and sense of humour, for instance, can apparently lead to acceptance of certain violent episodes, but not others (Gibson, 1999). Nevertheless, it would doubtless be attractive to many a moral campaigner to be able to ascribe direct 'cause' and 'effect' model relationships between media violence and aggressive behaviour, such as those that Ericson outlines in his excellent review article (1991: 220–1):

- the *hypodermic* model, i.e. 'a simple injection of media messages is said to result in a quick fix that affects attitudes and actions'; or

- the *cultivation* model, i.e. 'a sustained dose of bad material over a long period is said to result in a kind of symbolic addiction, with behavioural consequences'.

However, the research evidence accumulated over the years from laboratory and field experiments does not permit such neat, clear-cut conclusions. Most studies tend to be conducted within the positivistic psychological tradition (Reiner, 2000a) and Gauntlett (2001: 52–60) identifies a number of problems with the 'effects model' approach to the copycatting question:

- a tendency to tackle social problems 'backwards' – studies rarely use violent people as subjects, Hagell and Newburn's (1994) study of viewing effects on young offenders being a rare exception;

- 'superior' assumptions about children (and, for that matter, other mass audiences) who are typically treated as passive, unsophisticated 'non-judgmental dopes' (Garfinkel, 1967);

- studies are often underpinned by 'barely concealed conservative ideology', what Murdock (2001: 150) refers to as 'reservoirs of dogma';

- definitional problems – aggression is difficult to define and studies use widely differing parameters, ranging from physiological changes (e.g. raised blood pressure) in response to stimuli, to verbal abuse, through to observed physical assault on inanimate objects – clubbing a mannequin, for example;

- artificiality – experimental situations are often extremely contrived, determined in accordance with what Vine (1997) cautions is 'dangerous psycho-logic';

- methodological misapplications – a perennial hazard of correlational studies where confusion and conflation can result in erroneous assertions of causal relationships;

- selectivity – tendency to focus on popular fictional representations rather than news and factual outputs;

- ultimately, the effects model is atheoretical, being based largely on the kinds of questionable assumptions already identified.

As Reiner (2000a) notes, the search for the 'pure' media effect remains a 'chimerical' one and even where some findings of statistical significance do emerge, the conclusions that can be drawn from the vast output of the media effects research industry are often no more than 'masterpieces of inconsequentiality' (Reiner, 2000a: 53), the classic example of which surely remains that of Wilbur Schramm and his colleagues in their epic study, *Television in the Lives of Our Children*:

> For some children under some conditions, some television is harmful. For some children under the same conditions, or for the same children under other conditions, it may be beneficial. For most children, under most conditions, most television is probably neither particularly harmful nor beneficial. (Schramm *et al.*, 1961: 11)

Forty years on, Murdock (2001) dismissed the history of attempts to identify imitative effects as 'banal science'. However in his review of the literature, Ainsworth (1995: 89–90) did feel entitled to draw six tentative conclusions from findings about media effects:

1. Young children are more likely than adults to be influenced by on-screen behaviour.

2. Depictions of aggressors being rewarded for aggression seem more likely to be emulated than those in which aggression is punished.

3. Observing large amounts of violence may have a 'disinhibiting' effect which may lead to a lessening of individual restraint towards the use of violence.

4. Though watching violence may not induce violent behaviour, it may suggest new ways of inflicting harm.

5. Some kinds of violence committed by different people on screen may have a greater effect than others (violence carried out by 'goodies' appears more dangerous than the same act carried out by 'baddies').

6. Some 'personality types' may be more likely than others to imitate actions seen on screen.

Echoing the fourth point on Ainsworth's list, Howitt (1998: 79) also makes the observation that, in certain circumstances, the media may well shape the form of crimes, but that it does not determine criminal intent, which is why Gauntlett's call for more research on effects on offenders rather than hypothetical potential offenders may be more illuminating. Such research may 'inject a note of sanity into an increasingly hysterical debate', argue Hagell and Newburn (1997: 150), whose (admittedly small-scale) study found that the viewing preferences of delinquents are not markedly different from those for their age group in general.

For the moment, it seems that the safest conclusion that can be drawn is that while it is not possible to dismiss the media as having *nil* effects on criminal behaviour, the moral entrepreneurs' variously apoplectic and apocalyptic claims of *ill* effects are far from being firmly founded in fact. Incidentally, another 'effects' question rarely asked, but no less pertinent, concerns the 'effects' that media images of policing may have on the police themselves.

Fear of crime and the media

Fear of crime (FOC) has long been identified as a policy problem (Maxfield, 1984, 1987). How to measure it and how to ameliorate it continue to be debated. Cutting crime and fear of crime were identified as twin priorities by Tony Blair's Labour government, under which the Home Office was set the aim of ensuring by 2002, lower levels of worry for burglary, car crime and violence than in 1998 (Kershaw *et al.*, 2001). Initially the official response to fear of crime, based on the earliest British Crime Survey evidence, was to use data concerning the likelihood of a 'statistically average person' becoming a crime victim to allay people's concerns (Stanko, 2000). The aim of this 'administrative criminology' was to reassure the public by portraying the chances of being victimised as relatively remote, suggesting in the process that worries about crime (and by extension fearful members of the public, also) were quite irrational. At the same time, some critical criminologists were criticised for 'trivialising' crime and concerns about it (Young, 1997). So-called 'left idealist' criminologists began to be caricatured for their adherence to the position that, crudely put, as crime itself is a social construction having no ontological reality, *ipso facto* fear of crime is irrelevant: besides, crime should be viewed as essentially a proto-revolutionary act and, in any case, people cannot get enough of it in popular culture. However, 'left realist' criminologists such as Kinsey, Lea and Young (1986) took issue with both conservative administrative and left idealist approaches, each of which they argued tended to gloss over the differential distribution of crime and the impact of victimisation. Their local crime survey work on Merseyside and in Islington concluded that the higher levels of fear revealed in poorer neighbourhoods – especially in the inner cities – were not unrealistic, given the disproportionately higher rates of actual criminal victimisation there. The picture painted of women 'living under curfew' in some inner-city areas was, they argued, neither an unfounded panic reaction nor some nebulous non-entity but an accurate assessment of risk to their personal safety.

Like the imitative effects research mentioned above, studies of mass media and fear of crime point to a complex relationship, which must take into account a variety of variables including the medium, the type of programme involved (i.e. factual, fictional or factional) and the nature of the audience, who are in a real sense constantly 'commuting' between concerns around the various categories of media and crime coverage, and their concrete concerns about crime in everyday life (Reiner *et al.*, 2000b: 120). Differential viewing and reading habits must also be factored in, and cognisance given to questions such as 'do more fearful people read or watch more?' (Reiner *et al.*, 2000b: 109). Findings reported by Chadee (2001) suggest that the media, notably television, is a major source in influencing perceptions of crime. However, innovative qualitative research conducted by Roberts (2001) and colleagues, which made use of FOC 'diaries', appeared to show that media sources are perhaps less influential in promoting FOC than others have suggested. As they put it: 'overemphasis on violent crime in the national press tended to reinforce diarists' perceptions that their own localities were generally safe' (2001: 13). Jefferson and Hollway's biographical research on the risk–fear of crime paradox, confirms that experience and anxiety about risk, is 'never unmediated' (2000: 48). Research following in the tradition of Gerbner and Gross (1976) has continued to suggest that heavy viewing of crime drama can have such a mediating effect in the 'cultivation' of fear of crime, and may be associated with increased acceptance of tougher policing and penal policies (Cashmore, 1994; Howitt, 1998).

Also considered to be an important element in the media–FOC equation is the message sent and received with regard to the 'ending' of crime storylines in mediating audience reaction (Heath and Gilbert, 1996; Reith, 1999): some would argue that a denouement which features restoration of law and order may, for example, have a calming effect on the fearful viewer, while more open-ended messages about crime going undetected, unpunished and ultimately paying may be perceived quite differently. Related to this is a particular dilemma for the police, as psychologist Peter Ainsworth notes:

> One major danger which the police face when asking for the public's help is of alarming that public unnecessarily. There is something of a vicious circle here. The public expect the police to the solve the most serious and high profile cases; the police ask the public for their help in solving these crimes; the public come to believe that such cases are commonplace and become more fearful; society comes to believe that the streets have become unsafe; the public change their behaviour so as to feel less vulnerable; the same public then demands that the police should do more to make them feel safer, society also demands that more drastic measures should be taken against these people who are so terrorizing society. (1995: 206)

The reaction to the *News of the World*'s 'naming and shaming of paedophiles' campaign, instigated in July 2000 following the abduction and murder of eight-year-old Sarah Payne in Sussex, demonstrated precisely the sorts of dilemmas and demands that Ainsworth outlines. The paper launched a campaign to 'out' thousands of sex offenders throughout the UK, action that was supported by Sarah's parents Sara and Michael Payne, but condemned by senior police and probation officers as counter-productive (BBC Online, 2 August 2000). Summer street disturbances in the Paulsgrove housing estate outside Portsmouth were linked directly to the *News of the World*'s campaign and served to illustrate the dangers that distortion in media reporting on emotive crime issues can present (Garside, 2001). More recently, in relation to immigration and asylum, Howard (2001) detected an emphasis in press reportage on the 'language of illegality' and the imagery of 'feckless foreigners' (Jempson, 2001). Recognising that asylum seekers – and for that matter those mistaken for asylum seekers – are at risk of racially motivated attacks, the Association of Chief Police Officers produced in February 2001 a *Guide to Meeting the Policing Needs of Asylum Seekers and Refugees*, which called for accurate, informed and responsible media coverage of such issues (www.acpo.police.uk/policies/index.html). The outbursts of populist punitiveness unleashed in the wake of distressing cases and associated media campaigns prompted author Salman Rushdie to criticise the role of the media in promoting the cultivation of a lynch-mob mentality among readers: 'Something awful is happening here, some general degradation of public response caused by years of exposure to tabloid values' (Rushdie, 2001: 12).

The long-running and popular BBC TV programme *Crimewatch UK* consistently attracts a large and highly appreciative audience, but throughout its history there have been intermittent concerns about the ways in which it, too, sensationalises real crimes for entertainment purposes (Schlesinger and Tumber, 1993, 1994; see also Chapter 7). An important feature of the *Crimewatch* reconstruction is the tendency, as we have already discussed with regard to crime news, to focus on the most serious offences – homicide, armed robbery and sexual offences. Home Office ministers have been reported as blaming violent storylines in *Crimewatch* along with fictional television programmes such as *The Bill* for 'stoking fear of crime' (Wintour, 2000). Notwithstanding veteran presenter Nick Ross's reassuring 'don't have nightmares' message at the end of each show, there are understandable anxieties about the effects that its dramatic crime reconstructions might have on FOC levels. Citing an earlier research survey, Schlesinger and Tumber (1994: 267) recall that over 50 per cent of respondents said that watching *Crimewatch* increased their fear of crime, while a third said it made them 'feel afraid'. Williams and Dickinson's (1993) examination of the relationship between newspaper crime reporting and FOC was conducted in Sussex and involved quantitative analysis of space and prominence allocated to crime stories in ten national newspapers, qualitative analysis of crime reporting styles in these, and a questionnaire survey of the relationship between newspaper reporting and FOC. They found that more res-pondents attributed their fear of assault to TV or radio coverage (41 per cent) and press reports (39 per cent) than vicarious (11 per cent) or personal (4 per cent) experience and that, generally speaking, readers of the less 'fearful' and 'sensational' newspapers (quality broadsheets) demonstrated lower FOC levels than readers of tabloids (especially those of the 'low-market' variety).

While there does seem to be more substance for claims of linkages between mass media coverage and 'cultivated' fear of crime (Chiricos *et al.*, 1997) than for 'hypodermic' criminogenic effects, the bottom-line conclusion to be drawn from the literature on the former, appears no less equivocal than that of Schramm *et al.* in regard to the latter:

> The message is clear. Media messages do not affect all of the people all of the time, but some of the messages affect some of the people some of the time. As we move into an age of ever-expanding technological options in the mass media, we need to recognize that the process is as complex on the human side as it is on the technological side. (Heath and Gilbert, 1996: 385)

Conclusion

In spite of the attractiveness and persuasive appeal of many of the models mentioned in this chapter in respect of media contents and effects, definitive conclusions are difficult to reach. The best list that we can draw up from our own review of the literature and earlier syntheses comprises the following:

- The media-constructed image of crime is a 'false' one in that it tends to focus disproportionately on the serious, the sensational and the solved.

- While there are some qualified media 'effects' on audiences in relation to imitation of criminal behaviour, the research evidence does not support the definitive claims of causality sought after, or made by, many moral entrepreneurs.

- There appears to be slightly stronger evidence of 'cultivation' effects of the media on fearfulness of crime, but these are complex relationships with many dependent variables.

- Ultimately, mass media coverage does tend to be supportive of the police, representing and reproducing order through its underlying common-sense ideology about crime and policing.

- Concomitantly, the police may be correct in viewing the media as a threat because it raises unrealistic expectations about their detective abilities.

- However, the lack of emphasis in the media on unspectacular unrecorded, unsolved property crimes can be seen to let the police 'off the hook' for underperformance in such areas.

- Neither the 'subversive' nor the 'hegemonic' views of the media identified by Reiner (1997, 2000a) as ideal types can be rejected out of hand as being completely invalid.

Picking up on the latter point, it would appear that 'not proven' verdicts are more likely to be returned in trials of the media for subversion than in arraignments for hegemony. By their nature, charges of hegemony tend to revolve around conspiracy theories and, while it is substantially the case that the police do occupy a privileged position as 'primary definers', thus having the means and motive to ensure that a police-filtered version of crime news prevails, Reiner (1997: 225) is probably correct in asserting that the establishment including the police are these days having to work much harder for their hegemony, a fact that is reflected in the professionalisation of police–media relations which is the focus of our next chapter. In the final analysis, as Howitt concludes of media contents and effects, '[M]ore police and policing is the ideal solution to crime offered by the false media image of successful policing' (1998: 38). In the age of the Audit Commission, that will be music, doubtless, to many a cash-strapped contemporary chief constable's ears.

Chapter 3

Proceeding in a promotional direction

Introduction

Policing – and by extension police legitimacy – 'has always been as much a matter of image as of substance' (Reiner, 1994: 11). From the formation of the New Police in the nineteenth century to the Labour government's police reform agenda for the twenty-first (www.policereform.gov.uk), the police have been heavily involved in promoting themselves through 'image work', helpfully defined by R. C. Mawby as 'all the activities in which police forces engage and which construct and project images and meanings of policing' (2002: 5). As Reiner (2000b: ch. 1) summarises, the emergence of professional policing in Britain was at the time a highly charged and hotly contested political issue and, consequently, conscious efforts were made to develop an image which distanced the New Police from, on the one hand, the military and, on the other, the police of continental Europe (Emsley, 1996). On one level, this was to be achieved through the adoption of the blue uniform, an emphasis on civility, 'citizenship in uniform', and a mandate focused on patrol, prevention and preservation of the peace, discharged – in the main – without routine carrying of arms other than a wooden truncheon. In other words, this was essentially the birth of the 'brand' of the British bobby: unarmed, 'winning by appearing to lose' and 'a bastion to which people at every level look for reassurance and comfort' (Mark, 1977: 20). If not quite in tandem, there also evolved in Britain, against a background of deep suspicion and respectable fears about entrapment and other unsavoury practices associated with plain-clothes police on the continent, a detective branch, which succeeded in capturing both the imagination and support of the public. This admiring acceptance was due in no small measure to the depiction by journalists and popular authors (such as Charles Dickens) of a department characterised by devotion to duty, deductive reasoning and, increasingly over time, the appliance of science to the catching of criminals. As Rawlings notes:

> By the 1850s, two images of policing were emerging. The first was of the Bobby who was, depending on your point of view, tough but compassionate, or despised and feared, or a mixture of these. His main function was to prevent crime through the control of the streets and the imposition of a particular moral order. This was to be achieved by the exercise of the authority invested in the blue uniform. The second image was of the secretive and dramatic world of the detective and, in particular, the Scotland Yard detective, on whom most publicity was focused. He was entrusted with crime control through detection. (2002: 186)

As Reiner concludes, though it did not happen overnight, the combination of soft service and hard law enforcement inherent in these images was a formidable formula which bestowed upon the British police 'a unique character, implanting them firmly in national mythology' (Reiner, 2000b: 45), becoming and remaining, as Loader (1997) has noted, one of the principal means by which English society tells stories about itself. The duality of force and service is an enduring one (Stephens and Becker, 1994), which continues to provide a significant frame of reference for narratives about policing at a political level, in the news media, as well as in fictional programmes (Chapters 4 and 5). Tension between, on the one hand, the community safety role traditionally identified with the bobby on the beat and, on the other, the crime fighter function epitomised by the detective has brought both costs and benefits to the police over time, as they have begun to develop more proactive and purposive public relations approaches to shape the messages and meanings that attach to their various activities.

This chapter is concerned with exploring the dynamics of those inter-actions and the contexts within which they occur, with particular emphasis on the 'factual' news media. First, consideration is given to the nature of policework and news reporting, and how two seemingly different professions have perhaps more in common than is often acknowledged. Second, we consider the process of professionalisation of police–media relations, which has gathered apace since the 1980s when the traditional bipartisan consensus on law and order broke down and policing became for the first time a *party* political issue (Downes and

Morgan, 1997). Lastly and linked to that is the extent to which the police can be said to set the news agenda and, effectively, mould the message.

Policing and newsgathering – convergent construction work?

It could be argued that one of the constants of the police outlook is a sceptical disdain for journalists and the way that they cover law enforcement matters. For many police officers, the media are still frequently perceived as yet another hostile and unsympathetic quarter from which unjustified criticism can regularly be expected. The media are included in the ranks of the 'disarmers', whose capacity to undermine the police image makes them widely mistrusted in cop culture (Holdaway, 1983; Reiner, 2000b). There are certain ironies in this. First, as we have seen in Chapter 2, despite police misgivings about media (mis)representations of them, accumulated evidence from content analysis studies convincingly demonstrates that the way in which the police are presented in the press and other mass media is for the most part, a positive portrayal. As Reiner put it:

> The police are cast in the role they would want to see themselves in – as the 'thin blue line' between order and chaos, the protectors of the victimized weak from the depredations of the criminally vicious. The media … generally support the police role and even extensions of police powers. (2000b: 141)

A second irony resides in the fact that there exist a number of parallels between the job of journalist (in particular the crime and home affairs reporter) and the role of investigating officer. Each is under considerable pressure to 'get results' – in the case of the reporter to file the story, in the case of the detective to resolve the case. Neither is a stranger to long working hours, tight deadlines and difficult moral questions, nor to the stress that can accompany such an occupational mix. Both work within regulatory frameworks which, at times, can seem to consist of quite inhibitory, even downright obstructive legal rules: in the journalist's situation, the laws governing libel, secrecy and contempt; in the police context, the rules of evidence and disclosure. For both, their respective codes of practice and the *sub judice* rules can bring their own tricky and exasperating consequences, while the implications of the Human Rights Act 1998 in respect of privacy and autonomy of the individual promise to be considerable (Neville, 2000; Neyroud and Beckley, 2001; see also

Chapter 7). Both journalist and police officer well understand the frustrations of key witnesses being unprepared or unwilling to come forward and tell their story. Each is likely to have experienced encounters with abrasive lawyers and politicians and sundry uncooperative officials, including, on occasions, some from within their own organisations: the awkward editor or cost-cutting commander pulling the plug on an investigation by clamping down on expenses or overtime, for example. The dangers and dilemmas of handling informants and of working covertly provide further examples of common ground shared by both occupations.

Another important dimension of similarity relates to the impact of new technology, which is bringing profound changes to working practices within both the police and the news media. No one is suggesting for a minute that preventing and reducing crime and reporting the news are one and the same task, but as Ericson, Baranek and Chan (1991: 74) have suggested, there is a real sense in which 'the news media are as much an agency of policing as the law enforcement agencies whose activities and classifications they report on'. Electronic newsgathering and its global reach are having major effects both on the nature of news and on patterns of policing. Criminal events unfold as they happen in front of our very eyes, as 11 September 2001 brought home chillingly to the entire planet. The exponential growth in information and the ease with which ideas and knowledge can be disseminated internationally combine to blur conventional boundaries between the global and the local to give us what Bauman (1998) has referred to as the 'glocal' context. A good example of this tendency in relation to the transference of policing techniques and technologies is to be found in Boyle's (1999b) discussion of Strathclyde Police's reworking of the New York Police Department's 'zero tolerance policing' strategy. This high-profile approach to crime reduction was predicated on Wilson and Kelling's (1982) 'broken windows' theory which famously advocates tackling low-level, quality-of-life offences as a means of averting neighbourhood decline and more serious crime (Johnston, 1998). As Boyle observes, media relations were an integral part of the Operation Spotlight campaign. Throughout its duration, Strathclyde Police were constantly engaged in brokering news coverage and publicity that, on the one hand, promoted the potential of this type of initiative to cut crime dramatically as it apparently did in New York, while at the same time avoiding use of the term 'zero tolerance' by emphasising instead the local community context and the principle of individual street level officers exercising discretion and compassion. Boyle concluded that:

What Strathclyde police have identified is the importance of being aware of global shifts in policing, while attempting to remain sensitive to the needs of a range of local publics without whose support their job becomes impossible. (1999b: 247)

The use of the Internet as a means of chasing a story as well as pursuing offenders such as paedophile rings and terrorist networks is already well established (Neville, 2000; Allison, 2002) and, if Home Secretary David Blunkett has his way, the official police notebook may well be a thing of the past, as officers, like journalists before them, learn to love their laptops (www.policereform.gov.uk). The techniques used in evidence gathering and news gathering are increasingly similar: hand-held cameras are routinely used by the police for pre-event briefings, recording demonstrations and capturing crime scenes. At the same time, camcorders enable demonstrators and enthusiastic amateurs to turn the spotlight on the police, often generating sensational footage which in a real sense provides a twenty-first century response to the age old question of 'who watches the watchdogs' (see Chapter 7).

In our 'post-modern era of hypermediatization' (McLaughlin and Murji, 1998), the role of policing is inexorably shifting towards the assessment, management and documenting of risk, an enterprise that involves treading 'a fine line between public protection and public hysteria' (Neyroud, 1999: 15), as reactions to instances of 'naming and shaming' of sex offenders in the British media have amply borne out. In the 'risk society' in which everyone prepares for the worst (Beck, 1992; Johnston, 2000), the police, like programme-makers, are already among the key 'knowledge workers' (Ericson, 1994). Moreover, Ericson and Haggerty (1997: 140) have observed that 'in visually recording risk the police use the same technology as the news media and therefore can selectively supply the news media with material from CCTV and other footage'. Indeed, the rise of police 'infotainment' programmes might incline us a decade further on to invert Ericson *et al.*'s (1991) question to reflect the extent to which the *police* may have become an active agency in the selection and construction in this new media staple (see Chapter 7).

What is of particular interest is the crossover that exists between the nature of police work and the nature of news. Despite the apparent mutual antagonism and suspicion, what the police do and what makes news intersect significantly. This, in turn, drives a sense of dependency between police and members of the media, uneasy though this may be at times. The police are no longer the 'secret social service' that Maurice Punch referred to in 1979, thanks to four decades of (mainly participant observation) sociological studies and countless 'fly on the wall' TV documentaries on policing. Morgan and Newburn (1997: 79) captured the essence of the range and scope of policework:

> ... the police handle everything from unexpected childbirth, skid row alcoholics, drug addiction, emergency psychiatric cases, family fights, landlord–tenant disputes, and traffic violations, to occasional incidents of crime.

One might qualify 'occasional incidents' by referring to Shapland and Vagg's (1987) research finding that a significant amount of what the police do deal with can be said to be 'potential', if not actual, crime. The sheer range of activity and what Ian Loader (1997) refers to as the apparently 'insatiable public demand' for policing services, underlines the limitations of characterising 'core' policing as either crimefighting (as did effectively the 1993 White Paper on police reform (Home Office, 1993)) or community safety (as envisioned in the Crime and Disorder Act 1998. However, as R. I. Mawby (2000) has observed, while the existence of 'core' policing may have been exposed as a 'myth', it remains a seductive one, and one with which politicians, the media, the public and indeed the police themselves seem content to continue to flirt.

Like the reporter's lot, much of what the police do is mundane and routine, but in amongst that humdrum mix are dramatic events, compelling comedies and tearful tragedies of the human condition, which can provide the raw material of many a good news story. Consider Chibnall's classic checklist of eight news value imperatives (1977: 22–45) and how these might relate to the spectrum of police activity:

• *Immediacy* – news is about 'now' and more than ever it is a rolling '24-7' process, with bulletins requiring updates every 15 minutes or less. As Bourdieu put it (1998: 71), news is a 'highly perishable' commodity, and in the information age there is heightened pressure for members of the media to be the first and fastest with the freshest of stories. This pressure for immediacy accentuates the tendency that Chibnall identified for news to be about 'events rather than long-term processes'. Clearly the round the clock role of the police makes them one of the most accessible agencies to journalists seeking immediate comment and confirmation about intrinsically newsworthy events ranging from low-key demonstrations outside civic offices to serious road traffic accidents. As Innes notes, the police understand this dynamic only too well and know that in using the media during major criminal investigations, 'there are manifest benefits in doing so whilst the case is still a "hot" story' (1999: 284).

- *Dramatisation* – news favours the dramatic, or, as Chibnall put it, 'antics over argument'. From the street scuffle between 'neighbours from hell', through incidents involving domestic pets and other animals, to the splattered egg on a politician's suit, even if not in attendance or in close proximity, the police will generally be in possession of the 'facts' of the incident, thus underlining their value as an authoritative news source. However, as Chief Constable Elizabeth Neville, Chair of the ACPO Media Advisory Group, suggested, being too ready to assist the media with 'antics' stories (such as her cautionary tale of an escaped Malmesbury pig in Wiltshire, which attracted worldwide media attention) can sometimes backfire for the police if it becomes too 'hot' a story, which in turn leads to a media deluge (Neville, 2000).

- *Personalisation* – this has to do with the 'manufacturing' of fame and infamy, linked closely to the cult of the 'here today' celebrity, which is such an important ingredient in faction and the 'tabloidisation' of media, epitomised by the seemingly endless preoccupation with soapstars, pop idols, sports personalities and reality TV contestants (see also Chapter 7). Police involvement in cases involving even the most minor of celebrities caught up in traffic violations or criminal investigations whether as alleged perpetrators or victims are regular headline grabbers. High-profile police officers have found themselves becoming quasi-celebrities, a good example being former Super-intendent Ray Mallon of Cleveland Constabulary who earned the nickname of 'Robocop' for his uncompromising zero tolerance policing strategy in the North East (Johnston, 1998). Personalisation is closely linked to Chibnall's next tenet.

- *Simplification* – meaning 'whenever possible, social situations must be reduced to binary oppositions'. In the 1980s, as with 'hawks' versus 'doves' in US defence matters, there was for a while a tendency for British journalists to reduce policing to its 'soft' and 'hard' varieties, by deploying Devon and Cornwall's chief constable and community policing pioneer, John Alderson, to represent the former strand, while portraying James Anderton, the god-fearing, moralising chief of Greater Manchester as the embodiment of the latter. However, as Loader and Mulcahy (2001a, 2001b) chart, the 'cultural salience' of the 'hero' or 'maverick' chief officer has long since declined and these days the 'elite police voice' is more likely to be 'singing from the same hymn sheet' (Charman and Savage, 1998). Nonetheless, the variety of con-temporary policing voices (R. C. Mawby, 2002: 46–50) can be extremely helpful to journalists in this respect. For instance, the rank and file Police Federation's stance on a particular issue can often differ in emphasis from that of more senior officers and their staff associations, enabling complex matters such as firearms policy or aspects of police reform to be conveyed as simple contrasting opposites. Likewise, debates on criminal justice policy and punishment can be – and frequently are – readily simplified by juxtaposing a police point of view with that of a liberal pressure group or an academic criminologist.

- *Titillation* – as Ericson, Baranek and Chan put it, 'deviance is *the* defining characteristic of what journalists regard as newsworthy' (1987: 4) and few would dispute that sex, soaps and scandal do sell newspapers. In these days of the professional PR publicist, the police are frequently (and sometimes unwittingly and unwillingly) drawn in from the periphery to media circus centre stage when involved in investigating the kinds of incidents that have strong titillation potential. Witness, for instance, the stories in 2001 surrounding the discovery of a dead man's body at celebrity Michael Barrymore's home, and the bizarre and unfounded sexual assault allegations against the former Conservative MP Neil Hamilton and his wife Christine. Police scandals, particularly those concerning professional misconduct and sexual harassment within the organisation, also have headlining appeal, as a record number of very senior British police officers facing such allegations found out during 1998 (Mawby, 1999).

- *Conventionalism* – Chibnall refers here to the 'tendency for news events to be cast as well-known scenarios'. Thus we have a cast of familiar characters and labels used to construct a kind of e-fit 'common-sense' version of incidents: tragic victims, sneering death drivers, evil perverts, dedicated detectives, rogue cops, mindless thugs, ruthless drugs barons, all of which ensure that the focus remains on events and personalities rather than analysis of underlying causes and trends. As McLaughlin and Murji (1998) have argued, the Police Federation can bring to the news construction process a cluster of conventional 'storylines' about crime and policing which make the organisation not only a valued news source but also a formidable opponent in any public debate on police reform. Indeed it may well have been the Federation and its rich repository of 'storylines' that Eric Caines, a member of the Sheehy Inquiry (Home Office, 1993) had principally in his sights when he declared:

> Reforming the police is likely to be the toughest job of all. The police bodies are vocal and skilful operators and will mine every vein of public and political sympathy. (*The Guardian*, 2 July 1993)

- *Structured access* – news needs to be backed up by 'experts', therefore those with institutional legitimacy are granted privileged access to the media. Research in Britain and America confirms the status of the police as expert sources on crime and offending behaviour. According to Chibnall, a key feature in the development of crime journalism has been an increasing reliance on one major institutional source – the police. Schlesinger and Tumber's more recent study confirmed this, with journalists interviewed revealing that police made up anything between 70 and 90 per cent of all their contacts (1994: 162). Another significant development has been the rise of the specialist home/legal affairs reporter, concerned with criminal justice policy and processes as well as crime events and courtroom coverage, and thus perpetually looking for authoritative soundbites from the more articulate 'bobby lobby' which has emerged in the last twenty or so years.

- *Novelty* – the constant search for new angles. These days, police press officers typically have a canny nose for the novelty story and are generally happy to oblige with suitably amusing quotes from a police spokesperson to accentuate the angle. The police have also long been concerned with managing the appearance of effectiveness and innovation. As such, they are enthusiastic suppliers of novelty news surrounding their own latest gadgets and initiatives, like police patrolling on mountain bikes, roller-blading beat cops, not to mention the endless experiments with various new breeds of baton and sniffer dog. The acronym for the Home Office major enquiry computer system known as HOLMES remains a sub-editor's gift, especially if there happens to be in its vicinity a cop called Watson available for a photo opportunity.

The pressures and ideology that underpin Chibnall's checklist have, if anything, been intensified in the quarter century since it first appeared, not least as a result of the heightened requirement for immediacy in news. Over the same period the police have considerably professionalised their own approach to promoting themselves through the media, and it is to this aspect we now turn our attention.

The professionalisation of police–media relations

In our mass-mediated society, the police in common with most organisations in the public and private sectors increasingly view information and news management as being of crucial strategic importance. All

British forces now have media relations departments under a variety of titles, the majority of staff being civilians – including among them former journalists or marketing specialists (R. C. Mawby, 1999: 272). Increasingly, the police and constituent affiliates project a strong web presence and are constantly extending their range of 'e-policing' products and services to include, for example, the opportunity to report minor crime on-line and to register feedback about local policing issues (Leighton *et al.*, 2001). However, as R. C. Mawby (2002: 12) recounts, the police PR machine has developed from fairly rudimentary beginnings, the first police press office being, after all, a one-man band established in 1919 at Scotland Yard under the Commissionership of Sir Nevil Macready.

Relationships between police and press during the interwar years were in general somewhat fraught, though cordial relations did apparently exist between Metropolitan Commissioners and national newspaper editors. A key concern at the top was how to stem the flow of unauthorised leaks from further down the police hierarchy, and to preserve the force's reputation by keeping the lid on 'bad news' (R. C. Mawby, 2002: 13; Reiner, 2000b: 144). The golden age of crime reporting and the golden age of policing were co-located in the consensus mood of the immediate postwar years and an important figure in embedding and extending police–media relations activity was Sir Harold Scott, a senior civil servant appointed by Home Secretary Herbert Morrison to the Commissionership of the Metropolitan Police in 1945. Sir Harold is widely credited with promoting public confidence in the police through the maintenance of productive links with news outlets. Scott was also aware of the potential benefits of cooperating in the construction of fictional representations of police work, a factor attested to by the fulsome dedication to him and the police officers of the Metropolis in the opening credits of the 1950 Ealing film *The Blue Lamp* (see Chapter 4). These were still the days when, in the event of murders and other serious crimes, provincial forces, which were more numerous and smaller, called in 'the Yard' to assist in investigations. A pack of national newshounds would attach themselves to the London team – typically a detective superintendent and his sergeant – staying at the same hotel and receiving evening briefings over a beer in the bar (Schlesinger and Tumber, 1994: 155). As a result of this arrangement, some detectives, such as Robert Fabian, 'achieved superstar status' (Reiner, 2000b: 144) and became early models for lead characters in TV detective dramas (see Chapter 5).

The fluctuating fortunes of the police at the pens and keyboards of journalists since that quasi-mystical era up to the 1980s are captured in Reiner's (1989) four-phase periodisation of police research, which took account of journalistic as well as academic and official publications to gauge the mood of each shift. After the consensus of the late 1940s through to the end of the 1950s, came a 'controversy' stage, when a number of policing scandals surfaced, principally focusing on police malpractice and abuse of authority. Reiner (2000b: 59) notes that as we entered into the 1960s, we embark on the road to repoliticisation of the police and a period marked by highs and lows for the police image. The decade began with a Royal Commission on the Police, precipitated by a series of causes célèbres surrounding relationships between chief constables and local watch committees, and cases of incivility by more junior officers. The 1960s, however, saw some spectacular crimefighting successes, which gave the press much to praise the police for, notably the capture of the Krays and of the audacious Great Train Robbers. Police reorganisation was also reported positively. Amalgamations had the effect of ironing out the anomaly identified in the Royal Commission of 'admirals in charge of minesweepers', a reference to the standing (and doubtless sense of self-importance) of some provincial chief constables relative to the small size of their force establishments. A direct consequence of police reorganisation was a change in the status and tone of the elite police voice, which as Loader and Mulcahy (2001a, 2001b) note shifted from an essentially local focus to more of a preoccupation with the 'state of the nation', about which, for many old-fashioned chief constables, there was probably much to lament. The 1960s saw the arrival of mass TV ownership and an increasingly motorised society, developments that posed considerable challenges both to policing methods and police image work. A growing counter-culture was emerging, accentuating and accelerating the decline of the automatic deference to authority that had been the hallmark of 'golden age' postwar society. There were more and more diverse mass media images of policing around, coming at a time when TV drama was also being heavily influenced by American imports and the gritty kitchen sink realism of the British theatre plays of the so-called 'angry young men'. The original Z Cars was cast very much in this mould (Chapter 4), and the style of technology-led policing portrayed in it encapsulated what was happening in reality, namely a move away from more conventional forms of foot patrol and police–public interaction, to the unit beat system, which was to develop into a more reactive form of 'fire-brigade policing', which distanced the police from the public (Baldwin and Kinsey, 1982). Public confidence in policing was further undermined in the 1960s by a number of scandals concerning unethical detective work, among them the Sheffield Rhino Whip affair and the disturbing case of DS Harry Challenor in the Met (Reiner, 2000b: 60). With such malpractice exposés very much in the foreground, relations between the British police and the media were 'worsening at a time when wider interest in policing was developing' (R. C. Mawby, 2002: 18).

A climate of conflict continued throughout the 1970s. A cornucopia of corruption cases in the Metropolitan Police (Cox *et al.*, 1977; Emsley 1996: 179 *et seq.*), revelations about police violations of legal and civil rights, and a series of confrontations with middle-class sections of society 'fatally damaged the image of the police as impersonal and disciplined law enforcers' (Reiner, 2000b: 64). Although the golden age had gone forever, the decade saw positive changes in the way that the police – in particular the Metropolitan Police under Sir Robert Mark – opened up to the media. As Commissioner, Mark took on the twin challenges of cleaning up the 'fallen' Yard and improving the organisation's image and public standing. He is widely credited with turning around the paradigm of police–media relations from the days when disclosure of information was regarded as virtually an indictable offence, from 'tell them only what you must', to 'withhold what you must' (R. C. Mawby, 2002: 21). Under Mark, the Met's Press Bureau assumed a new strategic importance, and became a kind of role model for provincial forces and, as Mawby suggests, signalled the beginning of the 'embedding' of police–public relations. Mark's influence in the sphere, however, went beyond simply promoting the Met. As Loader and Mulcahy (2001b: 253) put it, Mark 'endeavoured to mobilize his peers around what one might call an *explicit theory of the chief constable as social commentator*' (emphasis in original). As mentioned above, the decade sees the rise to prominence of the outspoken chief constable, figures such as James Anderton, who had highly personalised media profiles and who, like Mark, made regular *ex cathedra* pronouncements on a whole range of social and constitutional matters. However, theirs was not the only police voice in the media. The 1970s also brought about a step-change in the politics of the police, notably in the form of the Police Federation's long-running law and order campaign. Launched in November 1975, this initiative culminated a fortnight before the 1979 general election with full-page national newspaper adverts which put forward an overtly conservative case for tougher penal policy and improved police pay and resources (McLaughlin and Murji, 1998).

Following the arrival of Margaret Thatcher and her first Conservative government, the British police entered the 1980s amid widespread suspicion that their role had altered irredeemably from impartial citizen in uniform to political partisanship. Soon after the election, the government implemented the Edmund-Davis pay formula (1979), while at the same time embarking on a sustained programme of cuts in other public services. As the 1980s progressed and industrial relations worsened, the Thatcherite philosophy that there was 'no such thing as society' took root.

The police found themselves in seemingly perpetual conflict with alienated and disaffected groups, from the 1981 urban riots in Brixton, Toxteth and Moss Side, through the Miners' Strike of 1984–85 to confrontations with hippie convoys in 1986. While initially media coverage of public order events was filmed through a 'law and order' lens, as Reiner (2000b: 146) observes, the discourse became ever more critical of the police. Many commentators feared a drift into 'paramilitary policing' (Alderson, 1998; Waddington, 1991) as the police on mainland Britain appeared to be intent on tooling up with the trappings and techniques more usually associated with the troubles in Northern Ireland or a continental *force de frappe*: riot gear, shields, water cannon, CS gas and plastic bullets. In this period of 'critical consensus', of necessity the police needed to handle the media in a more proactive way. It was widely recognised that the provision of facilities to journalists and other programme makers, such as pre-event briefings, interviews with suitable spokespersons and access for observation, photography and filming, would all be critical determinants in the way that the public perceived police handling of demonstrations and other public order situations. However, some forces displayed more savvy than others in this regard, as the varying coverage of picket line confrontations during the Miners' Strike illustrated only too vividly. In areas where more proactive media policies were pursued, filming tended to be shot mainly from behind police cordons, thus conveying images of the back of the 'thin blue line' straining bravely to maintain order in the face of abuse, in stark contrast to images of cavalry charges captured from behind the ranks of fleeing pickets.

While the police were for a while 'the talismanic public service' (Savage and Leishman, 1996: 245), this began to fade against a backdrop of continued expenditure squeezes and the rise of new public management in the public services. The process of change which began for the police with Home Office Circular 114/83 which demanded Value for Money in policing was to continue through the 1980s and into the 1990s with increasing pressure being applied from many quarters to improve the performance of what was beginning to be seen by many, including the Conservatives, as a failing force in need of fundamental reform. What Peter Manning (1997: 32) refers to 'the dramatic management of the appearance of effectiveness' becomes an organisational imperative and an important development in this respect followed the appointment of Sir Peter Imbert as Metropolitan Police Commissioner in 1987. Having already established strong media awareness credentials as Chief Constable of Thames Valley Police where he courageously allowed access to film-maker Roger Graef to make the path-breaking documentary *Police* in 1981, Imbert championed the cause of corporate communication in the Met. Consultants Wolff Olins were invited in to give the force a corporate identity makeover. As Mawby observes, the consequences were far-reaching: the need for a culture change was identified and intent to achieve this was signalled by a change of name from Metropolitan Police force to service and through the drawing up of a *Statement of Common Purpose and Values* that has provided a template for subsequent police Quality of Service initiatives elsewhere (Waters, 2000). As Schlesinger and Tumber (1994: 108) observe the PLUS programme also heralded the advent of more coherent corporate communications strategies in policing aimed at internal as well as external stakeholders.

From the early 1990s onwards, images of the police in the factual news media have been, as Reiner (2000b: 146) asserts, 'contradictory'. Critical coverage continued in respect of the denouements of the Hillsborough football stadium disaster of 1989, and of a long-running series of miscarriages of justice cases, championed by journalists like Chris Mullin and Paul Foot. At the same time, the deep-rooted sexism and institutionalised racism in policing were propelled to the fore by a number of high-profile industrial tribunal cases and, of course, the Stephen Lawrence Inquiry (Walklate, 2000). However, falling crime rates and, by comparison with the previous decade, relatively few public order confrontations assisted in the promotion of a 'counter-critical' message, even if the Audit Commission and Her Majesty's Inspectorate of Constabulary continued to raise questions about the effectiveness and efficiency of some police practices. In the aftermath of the lobbying and campaigning against the Sheehy Inquiry's recommendations in 1993, the various voices of the service seemed to have become less strident, less overtly 'political'. Instead, we can identify a more corporate approach to police promotionalism among chief constables, individual police services and the staff associations. In seeking to facilitate organisational change and the projection of their organisations' values, goals and missions, the incorporation of visual and corporate identity techniques such as the use of logos and PR consultants becomes widespread. The movement of senior Metropolitan officers – described by Schlesinger and Tumber (1994: 119) as 'media relations innovators' – to other large forces in England and Wales (such as Geoffrey Dear to the West Midlands, Richard Wells to South Yorkshire and Charles Pollard to Thames Valley) further catalyses the spread of good practice. More police officers receive training in media relations techniques locally and nationally and policies increasingly encourage direct or expert knowledge of an incident, case, problem or policy as the key criterion for selecting the most suitable person to offer a soundbite rather than relying on just seniority of rank.

The official police spokesperson is nowadays more likely to be a civilian rather than a serving officer. According to R. C. Mawby (2001: 45), over 90 per cent of police press office managers are civilians, as are over 85 per cent of all press office staff. This continuing professionalisation trend was further evident in the establishment in 1998 of the Association of Police Public Relations Officers (APPRO), whose chair Gillian Radcliffe is a strong advocate of proactive media relations strategies and of media relations officers becoming formal members of management teams in serious criminal investigations (Jenkins, 2000).

Promoting the police has grown remarkably in sophistication since 1919 and the 'brands' on offer have developed far beyond the simple duality of bobby and detective of the 1850s. The police now offer a range of services to the media, who can, for instance, readily access ACPO's Media Advisory Group Guidelines on topics such as policy on naming crime victims and the investigation of 'cold cases' (www.acpo.police.uk) or look up the Police Federation's website to find out where the organisation stands on a range of contemporary policing and criminal justice policy issues (www.policefederation.org.uk). The Internet provides the police with many useful opportunities to promote their activities, not least in terms of updating press releases and 'controlling the context' of such information (Dykehouse and Seigler, 2000). However, law enforcement organisations are well aware that providing a website is, of itself, not sufficient and we can anticipate the emergence of more interactive e-policing services in the early part of the twenty-first century (Leighton *et al.*, 2001).

Police sources continue to feed journalists with 'deep background' prior to trials to allow for stories to be ready to run immediately in the event of a guilty plea or verdict. Assistance with location filming is another growing area of image work: Strathclyde Police – home of *Taggart* – for example, has its own film liaison officer based at its Glasgow HQ (www.strathclyde.police.uk). In seeking to promote single-issue anti-crime campaigns, such as Operation Bumblebee (against burglary in the Metropolitan Police Service area) or Operation Blade (against the carrying of knives in Strathclyde), the police will seek to provide various 'pre-packaged' materials and offer facilities to film 'dawn raids': incidentally, the modern-day media ride-along has probably added a fresh dimension to the phrase 'going for a spin'. While the primary aims of such initiatives are public reassurance and, as mentioned above, 'the dramatic management of the appearance of effectiveness', police managers are also well aware of how conducive to good morale a 'good press' can be, not to mention the link with preserving high levels of public support. Chief Constable Graham Moore, for example, told *Police Review* of the 'energising' effect that West Yorkshire Police's Operation Target (aimed at tackling fear of crime) had had on his officers (Mulraney, 2001b).

As they endeavour to get their messages across to a diverse range of constituencies, police commanders are also very much aware of the limitations of relying on the mainstream media. Deputy Assistant Commissioner Mike Fuller, head of the Met's Operation Trident initiative aimed at reducing gun crime in the capital, acknowledged that 'guerilla marketing techniques' would be followed if the campaign was to succeed in reaching disaffected 15–25 year olds, noting:

> We are also discussing with the broadcasting authorities as to how we could legitimately broadcast our Trident murder appeals on pirate radio, which is the most popular medium for our target audience. (Fuller, 2001: 25)

From his research in Strathclyde, Boyle (1999a, 1999b) suggests that a developing area of police–media relations work involves pre-planned efforts to strategically place and refocus 'crime stories' in order to raise public awareness and, quite possibly, to shift the sole onus for solutions away from the police by, for example, presenting vandalism as environmental stories and substance abuse as primarily a health issue. For many commentators, such proactive approaches to moulding the message sound alarm bells and raise questions about the extent to which the police can actually set the media agenda.

Dominance or dependence?

The issue of 'structured access' mentioned above, coupled with the enduring appeal of traditional 'common-sense' conceptions of crime, constitute central foci in Stuart Hall et al.'s Policing the Crisis (1978), one of the most extensive discussions about 'moral panic', a thesis which had been developed by other criminologists earlier in the same decade, notably Stan Cohen (1972) and Jock Young (1971). Hall and his colleagues sought to explain the 'mugging epidemic' of the early 1970s, a phenomenon which, they argued, resulted in the conversion of traditional street offences into a virulent 'new strain of crime', which in media accounts came to be associated principally with young black male perpetrators, with consequent discernible effects on criminal justice policy – notably sentencing – and the way in which the police deployed their resources. For Hall et al., the part played in the news construction process by the utterances of so-called 'primary definers', in other words the authoritative 'experts' with privileged access to the media such as MPs, judges, chief police officers and spokespersons of the other staff associations, was absolutely critical. Not only does it shape a particular crime agenda, but also, they argue, it can lead to the emergence of more 'mutually reinforcing' relations between those experts who initially 'define' the parameters of a discourse and the media (the 'secondary definers') who reproduce and transform controversial topics into issues of major public and thus political concern. This conversion from controversy to concern may subsequently engender a sense of impending social crisis, thereby ultimately legitimating shifts towards more authoritarian modes of social control.

This analysis, which Ericson (1991) dubs the 'dominant ideology' thesis, is rooted in Gramscian theory and couched in the language of class struggle. While the analysis remains influential (see, for example, recent studies such as Wykes, 2001) and the empirical data presented in support persuasively demonstrate how 'weak and confused statistical evidence came to be converted into such hard and massively publicized facts and figures' (Hall *et al.*, 1978: 17), their approach has been criticised by a number of authors on the grounds that it tends to overstate the role of the media as 'passive' or 'instrumental' recipients and transmitters of 'dominant ideology' in the news construction process (Sparks, 1992: 23–4). Schlesinger and Tumber note that:

> The essentially structuralist approach of Hall *et al.*, however, is profoundly incurious about the processes whereby sources may engage in ideological conflict prior to or contemporaneous with the appearance of 'definitions' in the media. It therefore tends to ignore questions about how contestation over the presentation of information takes place within institutions and organizations reported by the media, as well as overlooking the concrete strategies pursued as they contend for space and time. (1994: 20)

Nonetheless, as R. C. Mawby (1999) suggests, the police as dominant party in media relations has become something of an 'orthodox' view which he suggests requires careful re-examination. Using a number of illustrative case studies from 1998 – in a sense a kind of *annus horribilis* for the British police image – Mawby pertinently questions the extent to which the police can in fact set the news agenda, particularly where the media are flexing their watchdog muscles. Furthermore, his own research, in particular his field work in South Yorkshire Police (R. C. Mawby, 2002), does reinforce Schlesinger and Tumber's argument about the omnipresence of negotiation and 'struggle for meaning', even in the most carefully orchestrated set piece news conference. Similarly, while Innes's (1999) study highlights ways in which the police seek instrumentally to use the media as an 'investigative resource', it is important to differentiate between situations where the police can exercise a considerable amount of 'control' over context and outcomes – such as *Crimewatch* appeals, for instance – and circumstances where journalists can actively hinder investigations by setting their own pace and direction in pursuit of stories, including the 'contamination of witnesses'. In this connection, Boyle (1999a, 1999b), like Innes, draws an important distinction between the possibly more dependent and hence compliant 'local' media and the more maverick 'hit and run' representatives of national or even international news media. Crandon and Dunne (1997: 91), however, incline to the view that, by virtue of the police's role as gatekeepers, media dependency is such that the relationship between them is 'symbiosis at least and vassalage of the media at most'. However, we are more persuaded by Mawby's 'equilibrium' thesis (2002: 190) as a way of reconceptualising the balance of power between the police and the media. The relationship is certainly a 'symbiosis of sorts' (Neville, 2000) but the orthodoxy that the police predominate does need to be more mindful of Innes's caveat that:

> The media is not necessarily a functionary of the police institution, it is a diverse industry with its own set of guiding principles and objectives. On many occasions the desires and the priorities of the media may be in direct opposition to those of the police. (1999: 273)

The pertinence of Martin Innes's observation was much in evidence during August 2002, as public, police and media attention in Britain and beyond became focused on the distressing disappearance of two ten-year-old girls, Holly Wells and Jessica Chapman, from the Cambridgeshire village of Soham. As Britain's biggest ever missing persons inquiry tragically transformed into an abduction and murder investigation, the interaction between police and media – perhaps unparalleled in terms of immediacy and unprecedented in intensity – demonstrated by turns the fact that control of context in unfolding major incidents is a fluid rather than a fixed phenomenon. At first praised for the professional way that the media was handled in terms of keeping the story in the public eye, Cambridgeshire Police soon came to experience the three 'E's' of police–media relations – expectation, exhortation and excoriation – that we outlined in the previous chapter. As a reflective editorial in the *Independent* (19 August 2002) put it:

The media began to categorise the participants as villains and heroes: whenever the police got something wrong, they were excoriated in terms that should have embarrassed the commentators (but won't).

The Soham case seemed to illustrate at critical points just how fine a line there exists between a police-led media story and a media-driven police investigation and, ultimately, how difficult it is to be definitive about who controls whom in such tragic circumstances.

When one moves beyond the 'factual' media to consider fictional and factional images of policing, as we do now, that diversity becomes increasingly important in terms of the way that policing is mediated for public consumption. We will revisit the 'dominance or dependence' question in our concluding chapter.

Part Two
Fictions

Chapter 4

Patrol, plods and coppers

Introduction

It is fitting that a discussion of fictional portrayals of policing should begin with *Dixon of Dock Green*, for no series has encapsulated the bobby on the beat more completely. So resonant was the image of PC George Dixon walking the beat in Paddington Green that it became a symbol for a particular style of policing. Clarke (1986) notes the headline in the *Financial Times* following inner-city riots across the country in 1981: 'We can't leave it to old George any more' (Clarke, 1986: 225), while Leishman (1995) similarly observes that Dixon was enlisted in a national Police Federation advertising campaign against the Sheehy Report on Police Reform in 1993:

> George Dixon would not recognise many aspects of modern police work, but he would still find there the old fashioned values of commitment, responsibility and team work. Because we are not prepared to sacrifice them. Not now, not in the future. (*Evening Standard*, 6 October 1993)

Dixon of Dock Green had a bizarre birth or, perhaps more accurately, reincarnation. George Dixon first appeared as police constable 693 of Paddington Green in the Ealing Studio film *The Blue Lamp* in 1950. The film opens with the shooting of an innocent bystander attempting to stop a robber escaping the oncoming police car. The voice-over leaves the audience in no doubt as to the film's agenda:

To this man, until today, the crime wave was nothing but a newspaper headline. What stands between the ordinary public and this outbreak of crime? What protection has the man in the street to this armed threat to his life and property? At the Old Bailey, Mr Justice Finnimore in passing sentence for a crime of robbery with violence gave this plain answer, 'this is perhaps another illustration of the disaster caused by insufficient numbers of police. I have no doubt that one of the best preventives of crime is the regular uniformed police officer on the beat.'

Dixon epitomised the solution to the postwar increase in crime, personified in the film by Dirk Bogarde as the tearaway spiv. *The Blue Lamp*, in this respect, was a typical example of Ealing Studio's output during the 1950s which 'tried to grasp the reality of England as a unity, a family structure, local solidarity and mutual responsibility writ large' (Barr, 1993: 85). Dixon's colleagues at the station reinforce the country's unity with police characters drawn from all four home countries. This device is subsequently used in the opening episode of *Z Cars*, 'Four of a Kind'.

The Blue Lamp's screenplay was written by a former police officer, T. E. B. Clarke, and received a BAFTA award for Best British Film. One film critic for *The Times* said:

It is not only foreigners who find the English policeman wonderful, and, in composing this tribute to him, The Ealing Studios are giving conscious expression to a general sentiment. (In Walker, 1997: 91)

In the scene which precedes the shooting, Dixon is seen giving directions, looking after a lost child and ticking off an illegal market trader: 'Come on son, you ought to know better.' Dixon is proud to be a policeman: the tea-drinking, cheery bobby patrolled the streets in his smart uniform, keeping the public safe from harm: 'He was a straight backed, straight-laced, straight-thinking man with all the virtues of a boy scout' (Clarke, 1983: 44).

However, Dixon survives only twenty minutes in the film, dying in hospital after being shot during an armed robbery at a cinema. His death comes as something of a shock: he is seen in the operating theatre, then lying unconscious with his wife at the bedside. Police colleagues are told he is making steady progress. Just as a recovery and return to the beat seems likely, a senior officer receives a call from the hospital that he has died. The shock is all the greater because up to this point in the film, crime has been portrayed as of a broadly petty nature: bylaw-breaking by street traders, a minor theft from a jeweller's shop, lost children and found dogs.

The mundane nature of the majority of crime in films like *The Blue Lamp* contrasted starkly with the representation of law enforcement and criminals that had emerged from Hollywood since the 1930s. In tracing the development of American film, Parker (1986) argues that there was a 'negotiated struggle and eventual convergence' (Parker, 1986: 146) between the film industry and the institutional regulators in the 1930s, heavily influenced by the Catholic Church. This process led to a shift from the exciting criminal character depicted in films like *Little Caesar* (1931), *The Public Enemy* (1931) and *Scarface* (1932) whom the church feared would be emulated by the young film audience. Parker argues that the audience were the decisive confluence where film industry and church met. Hollywood was forced to guess how the audience might react to their latest plots while the church guessed how the audience might be affected by them. The subsequent narratives and portrayals of criminal and law enforcer represented safe bets for both and the format was continually repeated:

> It is not unnatural for the boys of a country which has recently lost its frontier to be excited and stimulated by tales of danger and thrilling adventure. But it is certainly not right for such a spirit to be fanned up artificially by the engines of a sensational press…by the movies and by the other modern instruments of mob excitement. (Parker, 1936: 149)

This statement issued by the US Department of Justice in 1936 is further evidence of the increasing pressure from the government on film-makers. Combined with the introduction of the Hays Code in 1934 restricting the content of crime films, the heroic gangster was replaced with the heroic police officer. In response, the studios simply showed the same crimes from the other side of the law, most clearly illustrated by Hollywood's most famous gangster actors metamorphosing into cops, Edward G. Robinson (*Outside the Law*, 1930; *Little Caesar*, 1931; *Smart Money*, 1931) became cop Johnny Blake in *Bullets or Ballots* (1936) and James Cagney (*The Public Enemy*, 1931; *Blonde Crazy*, 1931; *The Mayor of Hell*, 1933) turned heroic G-Man Brick Davis out to avenge the murder of his best friend in *G-Men* (1935).

Reiner (1981) expresses concern over the gung-ho vigilantism adopted by police films throughout this period: 'All encouragement was given to violations of due process and contempt for the law by the supposed enforcers' (Reiner, 1981: 202). This was, however, welcomed by public and critics alike: *The Times* said *G-Men* engendered '...a feeling of respect for the men who are paid to die in the execution of necessary work' (Walker, 1997: 287).

The emergence of the G-Man film and the public support for it can, in part, be seen as a response to the social problems of the Great Depression in America at the time: crime, poverty and slum housing. The portrayal of law enforcement in the G-Man films was part of what Roffman and Purdy (1981: 160) term 'social problem films', represented by three stock characters: the fallen woman, the gangster and the convict. Prison films of the same period such as *I Am a Fugitive from a Chain Gang* (1932), *The Criminal Code* (1931) and *The Big House* (1930) offered a metaphor for social inequality and isolation within a disinterested institution:

> ...the films' evocation of innocence living in subjugation and terror clearly reflects the despair of the nation faced with incomprehensible social and economic upheaval...the cells and bars and chains eloquently re-create the sense of frustration and restriction in a land of lost opportunity. (Roffman and Purdy, 1981: 28)

Audiences could relate to the innocent man wrongly convicted who suffered injustices at the hands of the system in films such as *20,000 Years in Sing Sing* (1933) and *Each Dawn I Die* (1939). Similarly, the G-Man films offered a metaphor for public discontent during the recession in 1930s America: identifying the criminal who embodied the failure of the system, but more importantly, a solution in the shape of the heroic cop. British audiences, however, had a level of detachment from the gangsters and G-Men. These depictions of crime did not tally with the experience of a British public who viewed the police as residents in uniform. As Clarke (1983) points out, this common view shared by police and public alike was at the centre of *The Blue Lamp* and significantly it became the central tenet six years later for *Dixon of Dock Green*.

Such was the popularity of the character of George Dixon in *The Blue Lamp* that in 1956 the BBC resurrected him as the central figure in their police drama *Dixon of Dock Green*. The actor who played George Dixon, Jack Warner, was already over sixty when the series began and he continued up until the last episode in 1976. Written by Ted Willis, Dixon outlasted its appeal, in latter years appearing increasingly anachronistic alongside harder hitting police procedurals like *Z Cars* and *The Sweeney*. At its inception, however, *Dixon* represented a progression in authenticity for police drama. Reiner (1994) notes that where detective dramas such as

Dial 999 had championed the mystique of the sleuth, *Dixon* returned to the relatively mundane concept of community-based crime and criminals:

> *Dixon of Dock Green* was a novel departure in focussing on the comparatively humdrum routine of the foot-patrolling uniform constables and divisional CID of a local police station, not the serious crimes tackled by the elite squads that were the traditional grist of the TV cops and robbers mill. (Reiner, 1994: 22)

Community was at the very heart of *Dixon*, with George its main focus. On speaking terms with the local villains, they thankfully accepted arrest, grateful for the opportunity to see the error of their ways. Clarke (1983) points out that the apparent postwar unanimity between police and public was epitomised by the series: 'If the hegemonic ideal of government by consensus was ever achieved it was here in Dock Green in the fictional construction of the period of postwar reconstruction' (Clarke, 1983: 46). The locale of the series, Dock Green, represented the London East End, which as Laing (1991) notes, emphasised traditional working-class values reinforced by the programme's initial theme tune 'Maybe It's Because I'm a Londoner'.

In the fairy-tale world of Dock Green where honesty was the principal currency and crime never paid, PC George Dixon was the embodiment of all that was good and dependable. He was always immaculately turned out, resplendent in his tunic as he walked the beat. His desire to protect and serve his community was only matched by his concern for his family. The black-and-white ordered world of good versus evil, of simplistic morality, was reinforced in Dixon's monologue on the station steps under the blue lamp at the end of every episode. Years before Jerry Springer had his Final Thought, George Dixon would use the night's story as a reminder to the audience to stay on the straight and narrow. The avuncular, paternal style he showed to young coppers and tearaways alike was invoked to help the viewer help themselves, a style which divided the public over time: '...as a police officer at that time, and of course with many others, we liked the image that Dixon created and the message he always left behind' said Sir John Woodcock, former Chief Inspector of Constabulary (*Barlow, Regan, Pyall and Fancy* BBC 2, 1994). *The Times* was less impressed: 'Dixon's habit of presenting an explicit moral conclusion at the end of each episode tended to place Dixon and his doings just one degree further from reality than they can conveniently bear' (cited in Laing, 1991: 130).

The holistic nature of *Dixon*'s police work, dealing with families and troubled citizens as much as villainy, was reflected in its scheduling, broadcast as family viewing on Saturday evenings at 6.30 p.m. In this respect, the harsher crime control image presented in later police series like *The Sweeney* and *Cops* was preceded in *Dixon* by a caring approach. In his excellent periodisation of the genre, Reiner (1994) suggests that *Dixon of Dock Green* can be seen as the thesis in a dialectical analysis of the police procedural, the starting point from which all other police dramas should be studied:

> The thesis, represented by *Dixon*, presents the police primarily as carers, lightning rods for the postwar consensual climate. Its antithesis, *The Sweeney*, portrays the police primarily as controllers, heralding the upsurge of a tough law and order politics in the late 1970s. The synthesis, *The Bill*, suggests that care and control are interdependent, reinforcing each other. (Reiner, 1994: 20)

This analysis is discussed further in Chapter 6. One initial problem with Reiner's analysis is the relative neglect of *Z Cars*, the next major British television police series to emerge. In identifying the three dominant moments in the development of the police procedural as those above, Reiner diminishes the impact and importance of *Z Cars*. While he correctly recognises the significance of a series which radically challenged the 'Dixonian' depiction of the police in *Dixon*, he nonetheless pigeonholes *Z Cars* as a mere point of transition, a placement which will be reappraised.

From Toy Town to Newtown: *Z Cars*

As mentioned in Chapter 3, by the early 1960s, law and order and particularly policing had begun to re-enter the political arena. Downes and Morgan (1997) identify the Conservative Party manifesto of 1959 as the first time that a political party in Britain had overtly referred to the issue of crime in a political campaign. As the crime rate rose, there was increasing public concern about the safety of the streets. Clarke (1983) comments that the printed press were warning of a crime problem in London to match that of New York, and against this background the world of Dock Green was looking increasingly remote. In addition, the BBC had only half the viewing time enjoyed by ITV in what was proving to be an increasingly popular medium (Laing, 1991: 126). The new controller of BBC Television programming, Stuart Hood, looked to drama serials to address the viewing figure problem and a production team was assembled to create the first series of *Z Cars* which was to run for thirteen weeks.

For script writer Troy Kennedy-Martin and producer John McGrath, *Dixon* perpetuated a representation of the police and society that they wished to challenge:

> I wasn't interested in making another static series about the police. We wanted cars that moved, cars that moved from one bit of society to another but also we wanted very much to be able to break up those long scenes, those long boring moralistic scenes that television was full of. (John McGrath, in *Barlow, Regan, Pyall and Fancy*, BBC 2 1994)

There was also a desire to depart from the uncomplicated crimes that permeated *Dixon* and, as Troy Kennedy-Martin explained, to explore the difficulties of policing in the 1960s:

> Young policemen coping with problems that weren't cut and dried as you would think they might be in *Dixon of Dock Green*. So they were dealing with drunks who were old enough to be their father, intransigent problems with family. (*Barlow, Regan, Pyall and Fancy*, BBC 2, 1994)

McGrath and Kennedy-Martin looked to the US cop shows such as *Highway Patrol* to inject pace into the police procedural while 'getting into houses, into social matters' (Kennedy-Martin, *Without Walls: C4PD – Z Cars*, Channel Four, 1996). According to McGrath, *Z Cars* was not conceived as a police drama at all but as a documentary about people's lives:

> Something that will unfold in narrative form all the minor stories that make the fabric of our society so alive. Use cops, OK, but as a device for getting into the small but important realities of the lives of the people who are going to be watching. No master-criminals, super-sleuths, gentlemen experts, cunning detectives – the police are not our heroes: the people are the heroes. (McGrath, *Without Walls: C4PD – Z Cars*, Channel Four, 1996)

In production terms, *Z Cars* was a world away from the stately pace of *Dixon*. The early series, from 1962 to 1965, were shot live with six cameras. Filmed in a new BBC studio, the series utilised back projections and film footage. Laing describes the impact of this new approach: '…it blew away all the comfortable conventions of the old series like *Dixon*...This for people watching at home was new and exciting TV. It was like nothing they had ever seen before and that, at the end of the day, was the thing that made *Z Cars* so important' (Laing, in *Barlow, Regan, Pyall and Fancy*, BBC 2, 1994).

Z Cars was set in the fictional estate of Newtown, loosely based on Kirkby outside Liverpool. The *Radio Times* explained the significance of the location in its preview of the opening episode: 'Life is fraught with danger for policemen in the North of England overspill estate called Newtown. Here a mixed community, displaced from larger towns by slum clearance, has been brought together and housed on an estate without amenities and without community feeling' (cited in Laing, 1991: 129). Newtown, and a second community in Seaport, were given a quasi-Wild West reputation, epitomised by frequent punch-ups in the local Tabernacle pub and a distinct lack of community feeling. There was also an attempt to reflect changes in police approaches to crime during the 1960s, with the advent of the panda car used in tandem with foot patrol; community policing, so prevalent in *Dixon*, was replaced by the unit beat system. Leishman (1995) notes that Lancashire was one of the areas used as a test-bed for these new types of policing, thus allowing *Z Cars* to develop its distinctive content and format.

The first episode of *Z Cars* was broadcast at 8.30 p.m. on Tuesday, 2 January 1962. 'Four of a Kind' introduced the audience to the characters and the setting for the series. Echoing the opening of *The Blue Lamp*, the first episode makes constant reference to the rise in crime and the lack of police resources: 'Factories going up, these new estates, new towns mushrooming up like the plague, full of thieves, tearaways and villains. Now a PC gets murdered' (Detective Inspector Charlie Barlow in 'Four of a Kind'). The dead policeman, PC Farrow, was murdered in the execution of his duty, the opening scene of 'Four of a Kind' showing Barlow visiting Farrow's grave. His frustration over the scarce manpower at his disposal is used to introduce the audience to the crime car, central to the *Z Cars* format.

Sergeant John Watt was to be in charge of the two crime cars which patrol Newtown and his brief for selecting suitable officers was explained to him by the grittily Northern Chief Superintendent: 'Get keen young lads with a knack for catching thieves. That's what we want. I don't care what they look like, but get 'em hard'. The progression from foot patrol to crime car, the frequent references to violence and the senior officer's penchant for coppers who could handle themselves woke the Dock Green audience from their cosy slumber and dragged them into the hardened anomic world of mid-1960s Liverpool. The transformation from old to new and the ensuing struggle to introduce new police strategies and technology is articulated in the words of Dixonian desk Sergeant Twentyman: 'It's on the beat you need your men, it's on the beat you keep the peace…not escaping into fancy cars'.

And so the two crime cars, pictured in the opening titles as the eyes and ears of Newtown nick, arrived. Zed Victor One featured the artful Irishman Lynch and the ambitious Home Counties copper Steele. Both men, however, fall a long way short of the moral standards set by George Dixon: Lynch is depicted as a 'lady's man' and uses the police telephone to check on the odds for his horses, while Steele argues with his wife, Jayne, who has a black eye received in retaliation for throwing a hotpot supper at him. In Zed Victor Two rode 'Fancy' Smith, an imposing Lancastrian, who explains to two young girls attempting to get into a nightclub, 'Anyone who spoils my patch with trouble gets the back of my hand'. His partner was dour Scotsman Jock Weir, introduced to the audience on a stretcher semi-conscious after a rugby match. Assuring his superiors of Weir's suitability for the job, Watt tells them 'He can handle himself in a bundle'.

The themes in 'Four of a Kind' set the tone for the rest of the series: an overworked and under-resourced police force battling against the growth in violent crime in a sprawling, disordered community; four young officers attempting to cope with situations they had not previously encountered; problems that will never be solved with a cheery 'evening all' and a hackneyed homily under the reassuring hue of the blue police lamp: 'The iconoclasm of Z Cars lay in its warts and all portrayal of the police as adults with personal weaknesses and defects, rather than the Dixonesque superannuated boy scout image' (Reiner, 1994: 22–3). While the series was hailed as a success, critically acclaimed as 'realistic to a fault' (The Times, cited in Laing, 1991: 130), some senior officers were incensed. An oft-quoted incident concerned the then Chief Constable of Lancashire, Eric St Johnston, driving down to London to confront the BBC Controller of Programming after the broadcast of 'Four of a Kind', demanding that it be taken off air. The former Chief Inspector of Constabulary, Sir John Woodcock, reiterated these sentiments:

> When Z Cars came along we were really dismayed that they'd portrayed a police officer as being brutish and violent, and violent domestically as well as in relation to duties. (Barlow, Regan, Pyall and Fancy, BBC 2, 1994)

As the first series progressed, the BBC found itself with two contrasting police series both attracting high audience figures. While Z Cars challenged the rather too-good-to-be-true world of Dock Green, *Dixon* still continued to attract followers. Laing (1991) traced viewer opinions on both series in the letters pages of the *Radio Times* from the period and notes support for both series: 'If Dock Green (which reminds me of a social club) is authentic I am not surprised at the high rate of crime in this country…there is nothing phoney about *Z Cars*' (Laing, 1991: 131), wrote one viewer, while Lady Saville of London SW7 wrote in March 1962:

> The actors in *Z Cars* are good, but they never for one moment give me the impression that they are anything but actors, whereas the cast in *Dock Green* especially Flint and Dixon seem to be utterly and entirely genuine policemen. (Laing, 1991: 129)

It is interesting to note that the success of *Z Cars* is judged on how 'realistic' it is. As discussed in Chapter 1, the relationship between police drama and policing in the 'real world' is a complex one. The representations of the police in *Z Cars* are a negotiation between audience knowledge of the police, previous police shows like *Dixon* and *Highway Patrol* and elements of real policing in the 1960s. Even though it put the police in panda cars, *Z Cars* still focused on the battle for doing what was right, of protecting a community *and* struggling against a rising tide of crime with decreasing funding and personnel.

There is also a constraint on format, justice is meted out by the police at the point of arrest: there are no court hearings nor prison scenes. Hurd (1981) argues that this has particular significance in relation to characterisation, suggesting that characters and their actions are 'the carriers of meaning' (Hurd, 1981: 58). Primarily, this manifests itself in a hierarchy of characters with the police at the top. This is achieved through the regular appearance of the main police officers played by recognisable actors. In *Z Cars* these were Barlow (Stratford Johns), Watt (Frank Windsor), Fancy (Brian Blessed), Lynch (James Ellis), Weir (Joseph Brady) and Steele (Jeremy Kemp, later replaced by Colin Welland).

This is in contrast to criminals who are often played by actors in cameo roles who have to rely on crude stereotyping to make themselves immediately identifiable to the audience: 'villainy is rendered amorphous, abstract, perhaps anonymous' (Hurd, 1981: 58). Such forms of stereotyping are achieved via clothes and physical characteristics, or through particular behavioural patterns such as violence, disloyalty and cowardice. In *Z Cars* the villain is frequently comic: the drunk driver in 'Friday Night': 'I refuse to be examined for drunkenness without my doctor being present and he's on holiday in The Canaries'; or grotesque: the pornographer (played by Joss Ackland) selling his wares to children in 'Happy Families'. Hurd identifies two stereotypes in the portrayal of the criminal in *Z Cars*: the apprentice criminals from rough home backgrounds and stereotyped members of the public exemplified by the patronising aristocrat and the uninformed pedantic councillor.

Dominick (1973) has suggested a reason for such an imbalance in characterisation. He argues that in presenting crime and criminals, there is an attempt not to vilify or malign certain groups in society. Yet each crime must have someone to perform it, someone who is victimised by it and someone to track the criminal down and bring him/her to justice. Therefore in an attempt to avoid charges of racial or ethnic stereotyping, television producers have made criminals as non-descript as possible. Therefore, 'a television criminal is a function not a person. He exists solely as a criminal, his character is seldom developed any further. He is a one-dimensional caricature, carefully drawn to be as inoffensive as possible' (Dominick, 1973: 249).

Criminal stereotyping strengthens the police position vis-à-vis the criminal. Contrasting the fully rounded police character with the superficial cardboard cut-out offender strongly suggests the notion of ultimate police supremacy and infallibility. As we have discussed in Chapter 2, this resonates with Hurd's notions of a 'preferred reading' and of reality and authenticity producing meaning, namely a social construct of the police favourable to them.

The concept that regular characters carry meaning has been further developed by Hurd in a discussion of the narrative structure of the police procedural. *Z Cars*, Hurd argues, is a decentred biography in which the social world of the police comprises individual relationships between the police and the public: 'policing is not the organised institution of social control of which policemen are the agents but is translated exclusively in terms of face-to-face relationships of open eyeball to eyeball confrontation...' (Hurd, 1981: 64). A few examples will suffice. In 'Happy Families' (1964) we see Inspector Barlow snarling at pornographer Shields: 'I believe you, I believe you're stupid as well as vicious and depraved'. In 'Friday Night' (1962) Bob Steele watches a motorcyclist die in his arms while awaiting an ambulance and in 'Handle With Care' (1962) Fancy Smith implores local villain Jake (Arthur Lowe) to tell him where he has hidden some stolen gelignite ('It might go off in a crowd or near a school').

In 1962 Kennedy-Martin and McGrath resigned from the show. The two felt that it had moved away from dealing with the difficult community-centred issues, which were replaced by narratives centred on the police characters. Kennedy-Martin was succeeded by John Hopkins, whose influence on *Z Cars* Laing describes as 'most significant...in maintaining and developing the programme's established style and standards' (Laing, 1991: 135). Hopkins himself felt that the interaction between officers and the public they served was central to Z Cars: 'The way the daily involvement with the public affected the police, how it changed, why they were police, all of this' (*Barlow, Regan, Pyall and Fancy*, BBC 2, 1994). Hopkins left in 1964 and by the end of 1965 falling viewing figures led to Z Cars being taken off air. Although Z Cars did not return in its live format, the series was revived in 1967 as a pre-recorded drama series which ran until 1978.

In Reiner's analysis of the police procedural, Z Cars is merely transitional – 'it prefigures the subsequent developments of *The Sweeney* in its profanation of the police series' (Reiner, 1994: 23). While this appraisal follows Reiner's argument of the police drama moving from the caring role of the police portrayed in *Dixon of Dock Green* to the crime control perspective of *The Sweeney* and the synthesis of the two in *The Bill*, the approach limits analysis on a care/control axis. Z Cars was more important than that. As we have seen, Z Cars' communicative design, thematic development and visuals were in stark contrast to anything that had gone before:

> Z Cars made a tremendous impact. It was very different because of the regional speech and location. This was a new world emerging from outside London, from a real working England. (Laing, in *Barlow, Regan, Pyall and Fancy*, BBC 2 1994)

The British bobby was no longer the embodiment of all that was good and proper; the police instead became altogether more human with faults and weaknesses. Society was not the rosy world of Dock Green but an environment in which crime was just one of the many problems faced by families and individuals.

In terms of television drama, the series introduced mobility, speed and a gritty authenticity in the new wave tradition of British films like *Saturday Night, Sunday Morning* (1960) and *A Taste of Honey* (1961). As one television critic elucidated: 'You can trace a line from Z Cars to all the successful contemporary television dramas in Britain because of this insistence on having people speaking fast and slangy and interrupting each other – not the kind of set speeches we'd had previously in television drama' (Hilary Kingsley, *Without Walls: C4PD – Z Cars*, Channel Four, 1996).

After Z Cars was taken off air in 1965, the characters of Detective Inspector Charlie Barlow and Detective Sergeant John Watt had proved so popular with audiences that they were retained for a new series, *Softly*

Softly (later titled *Softly Softly: Task Force*), which began transmission in 1965 and ran until 1970. Even after the end of the series, Barlow continued in two of his own series, *Barlow at Large* (broadcast between 1971 and 1973) and *Barlow* (1974–76). The two were reunited in 1973, when they disinterred the case files connected with the real-life 'Jack the Ripper' murders of the 1880s. This was later developed into *Second Verdict* (1976), another short series in which the two fictional characters investigated unsolved murder cases from real life.

Gentler touches

Although there were other developments in police drama in the 1970s – *New Scotland Yard* (1972–74), *Law and Order* (1978), *Strangers* (1978–82) and most notably *The Sweeney* (1974–78), and shows such as *The Growing Pains of PC Penrose* (1975) (later *Rosie* (1977–81)) where the police station provided a backing for situation comedy – it was not until 1980 that a new, substantial series concerned with foot patrol policing emerged.

In August 1980, Ian Kennedy-Martin, brother of *Z Cars* writer Troy, created *Juliet Bravo*, a police procedural in the style of *Dixon of Dock Green*, which was also broadcast early on Saturday evenings. The series featured Inspector Jean Darblay (later succeeded by Inspector Kate Longton) who takes control of a small police station in Hartley, Lancashire. The series, along with *The Gentle Touch*, was the first to depict women in senior police roles. Up to this point, women had been 'denied character either within or outside the social world of the police' (Hurd, 1981: 59). In *Z Cars*, Hurd argues that female characters were depicted as victims: as the mother receiving the news about her delinquent child from a policeman, or a wife duped by her criminal husband; while female police officers rarely developed beyond standing in the background of the interview room, police station or family home. In *The Sweeney*, women characters performed essentially the functions often seen in Hollywood films: 'The vamp, career girl, moll and mother' (Hurd, 1981: 59). *Juliet Bravo* and *The Gentle Touch* challenged these stereotypes, creating a new female perspective in crime drama. In Reiner's (1994) dialectical analysis, these two series paved the way for the shift from *The Sweeney* to *The Bill*: from a crime control agenda to a more caring approach. As Clarke (1986) notes, the transformation from the ferocious battles between villain and copper was, in part, due to the use of women in key roles which 'defuses the presentation of violence by overlaying and legitimising a caring dimension to the work of the police officer' (Clarke, 1990: 248).

A second development in the police drama at this time was the role of family. In both series, the narrative explores the relationship between the police officer and her family. In *Juliet Bravo*, the 'married to the job' theme is turned on its head while in *The Gentle Touch*, Maggie Forbes must cope as a single mother after her police officer partner is killed.

A key feature of *Juliet Bravo* was its emphasis on procedural accuracy. As Clarke (1987) notes:

> In *Juliet Bravo* it is expected that people will be interested in the detail of police work – 'documentary' accuracy over things like uniforms is very important – and that *learning* how a particular crime is solved is the reward for the audience. (Clarke, 1987: 36)

This quasi-documentary approach was developed and adopted *in extremis* by the most recent police drama concerned with the bobby on the beat, *Cops*. Arguably, however, the most accomplished exponent of this approach has been *The Bill*, which marked a significant progression in the representation of the police on the beat.

Fitting *The Bill*

As suggested in Chapter 3, throughout the early 1980s, the police were increasingly visible in the mass media following significant events relating to public order and security. In April 1980, riots broke out in the St Paul's area of Bristol attracting headlines such as 'Mob Fury – Looting and Fires as Riot Erupts' (*Daily Mirror*, 2 April 1980: 1). In 1981, there were further disturbances in Southall, Brixton, Toxteth, Moss Side, Handsworth, Sheffield, Nottingham and Hull. The conviction of Peter Sutcliffe later that year also raised questions about police competence during murder investigations. In 1983, police mistakenly shot Stephen Waldorf believing him to be an armed robber and in 1984 WPC Yvonne Fletcher was shot, killed by machine gun fire outside the Libyan Embassy in London. There were also several chief constables with a high profile in the media, notably John Alderson, and James Anderton. The increased public awareness of policing in Britain at this time helped to create the demand for a new police series that reflected some of the issues that had been raised by these events.

The form and structure of this series, however, was to be influenced by Roger Graef's 1982 documentary *Police:* a seminal and ground-breaking fly-on-the-wall examination of the Thames Valley police force. The bumpy camera work and police perspective were adopted by script writer Geoff McQueen who had written a trilogy of plays dealing with the police, the first of which, *Woodentop*, was broadcast on 16 August 1983. Peter Creegan (who had previously worked on episodes of *Z Cars* and *Juliet Bravo*) directed *Woodentop* using a hand-held camera:

> It wasn't shot dramatically, as a film would be…I felt that the compulsion to view should come from the dramatic situations as written, and from the way in which the police dealt with them. The camera was there simply to observe all of this as it happened. (Lynch, 1992: 14)

The play became the basis for a new police series, *The Bill*, first broadcast on 16 October 1984. The series ran in one-hour slots until 1988 when it became a twice weekly half hour show. It increased to three shows a week before reverting back to once-a-week, hourly shows in 1998. More recently, *The* (new) *Bill* has appeared twice-weekly with occasional two-hour specials.

The Bill is essentially a police soap opera, 'telling everyday tales of constabulary folk' (Reiner, 1994: 27). Despite the changes in running time over its 15-year history, its format and structure have remained more or less consistent. The multi-layered narrative, involving several stories and departments within Sun Hill police station, has altered little since *Woodentop*. Each episode opens with an incident of one kind or another to catch the audience's attention immediately: for example, a disturbance at a party ('The Night Watch'); a thief returning stolen goods to his victim ('Revenge'); or a woman giving birth in an alleyway ('Soft Talking'). However, this incident is more often than not shrouded in mystery; there is either more to it than meets the eye or the incident itself is somewhat vague and ambiguous. The first scene cuts back either to the station or to a familiar scene such as a constable walking the beat. These nebulous beginnings lead to an unfolding of the narrative, often with two or three disparate events joining together before the commercial break leaving the audience to ponder the where? how? and who?

The narrative structure is supported by the point of view of *The Bill*. Unlike police shows that had gone before, every scene in *The Bill* has a police officer in it, emphasising the 'pseudo-documentary' feel of the series:

> We not only see the action largely through police eyes, but also from the police point of view and the audience is invited to 'put themselves in the subjects' place' and to take on their angle of vision. (Murdock, 1982: 21)

This is an important tool in the construction of the programme's representation of the police. In following the methods used in documentaries, *The Bill* takes on many of the former's characteristics: the shakey camera work, the warts and all presentation and the police perspective.

Despite these changes in perspective and format, much in *The Bill* is familiar from previous series. Hurd's notion of decentered biography discussed in relation to *Z Cars* is present in *The Bill* where team work is visually underscored by recurrent shots of Sun Hill: desk sergeant, police cells, interview room and CAD (Computer Aided Dispatch) room. In the piecing together of the crime, the audience often observes CID and uniform officers working together: in 'Whispers' CID officers stake out a suspect linked to a car crash being investigated by two PCs, while in 'The Chase' there is a call for 'all units' to tail a getaway car from an armed robbery.

The heritage of police drama is evident in *The Bill* in two long-standing characters from the series in the 1980s and early 1990s who were direct descendants from earlier police procedurals. Sergeant Bob Cryer was an updated George Dixon. Although considerably younger, Cryer had the same friendly nature, paternal concern for fellow officers and the public, and a similarly strong sense of what was morally right. The warm welcome back he receives in 'Decisions' following his wounding by a criminal with a police rifle also echoes the death of Dixon in *The Blue Lamp*. Cryer's colleague, Detective Inspector Frank Burnside, was an anachronism straight out of *The Sweeney*, the action-based cop show from the 1970s (see Chapter 5). In order to fit into the precise framework created for *The Bill*, Burnside had to be a 'watered down' version of *The Sweeney*'s Jack Regan, as too much illegality and violence would have been out of step with the ideology underpinning the series. Burnside was a hardened cynic with no room for sentimentality. During 'Rites', his colleague WDC Martella is concerned that a CID operation will overrun and make them late for the funeral service. Burnside replies:

> One thing at a time, eh! We've got enough on our plate without worrying about funerals…if I'd known you were that worried about it I'd've taken an ad out in *The Standard*; *would all villains please note, there will be no criminal activity on the afternoon of 27th*…well they aint got no respect 'ave they?

Despite this, he is like Regan, in Clarke's words, 'honest and incorruptible, firm but fair' (Clarke, 1986: 226) in possessing the street sense of 1970s thief-takers like Regan and Carter and a hard edge absent in everyone else during his reign at Sun Hill.

These two characters provide an overt link between *The Bill* and previous police dramas, 'linking police heroes across time, reinforcing the trust placed in the police' (Clarke, 1986: 226–7). There are further connections to the recent past with the procedural accuracy developed in *Juliet Bravo* and *The Gentle Touch* given even greater priority in *The Bill*. This can be partially explained by the introduction of the Police and Criminal Evidence Act 1984 but also by the desire to maintain the documentary production values exhibited in Graef's *Police* in 1982. Consequently, interview scenes are often accompanied by reference to official interview procedure: 'Behind me is a tape recorder, when you're ready the recorder will be switched on, we'll introduce ourselves, state the date, time and remind you of the caution then we'll begin, OK?' (PC Garfield in 'Growing Pains'). The Custody Sergeant is regularly seen undertaking the same line of questioning, asking for age, date of birth, address and surname. There are also real-life police posters on the Sun Hill noticeboards, featuring actual police initiatives like Operation Bumblebee. This attention to detail is stressed by the producer and other programme executives, according to one script writer.[1] The basis for this, it was suggested, is to ensure the continuing cooperation of the police for the series. Procedural accuracy also allows poetic licence in other areas. The volume of incidents at the station, for example, is far beyond the number that would occur in real life, but because of the foundation of procedural accuracy, the programme remains 'believable'. This echoes our discussion in Chapter 2 on the media's over-inflation of police success.

The Bill is fast becoming the most popular police drama of all time, rivalling *Dixon of Dock Green* for longevity and *Z Cars* for viewing figures. It both shapes police dramas that follow it and is shaped by those that went before it. In this cycle of continual evolution and retrospection, the British police procedural may have reached its final destination, in the shape of *Cops*.

More friends from the North: *Cops*

Cops was first broadcast in October 1998 and brought us back to familiar territory, a fictional police station, Stanton in Lancashire, where officers are shown to be dealing with escalating crime in a disaffected community. Nevertheless, its representation of the police was, in some respects, a departure from the police procedurals discussed so far. The communicative design of the series was based on the recent, and successful, form of the fly-on-the-wall documentary dubbed 'docu-soap'.

Such programmes as *Driving School, Airport, Paddington Green, Lakesiders, Clampers* and *The Adelphi*, which centre on groups of people in particular environments, use shakey hand-held cameras, often out of focus, and uneven sound. This same format was utilised by *Cops* in its depiction of policing, which blurred fiction and documentary. *The Sun* called it 'some horrific home video…horrendously squalid and terrifyingly real' (*The Sun*, 20 October 2000). Producer Tony Garnett, himself an actor in *Dixon of Dock Green* and *Z Cars* and producer of two other influential police series, *Between the Lines* and *Law and Order*, describes this approach as 'distilled naturalism' (Graham, 1999: 22), a form of eavesdropping on real life. The docu-soap approach is underscored by the lack of a title sequence, complete absence of incidental music, a cast of unknown actors and, perhaps most tellingly, by the narrative structure of the series. There is no dominant story in *Cops*, simply a number of events and incidents at which police officers are seen attending. Unlike *The Bill* these stories do not neatly overlap but run concurrently, cut together in a jolting manner moving us from one scene to another without overt explanation. Notwithstanding the production techniques, *Cops* in many ways resembles *Z Cars*, the policing problems of Newtown and Seaport in the 1960s become those of the Skeetsmoor Estate. The audience witnesses PC Roy Bramell talking plainly yet sympathetically to residents on his beat just as Fancy Smith would have done. The difficulties of juggling home lives and police work are no less difficult for WPCs Draper and Metcalf than they were for Sergeant John Watt. There are other parallels too. The first episode of *Cops* caused disquiet among police ranks in the same way 'Four of a Kind' did 36 years earlier.

In *Cops*, the opening scene has a young woman snorting cocaine in a nightclub toilet and then, realising she is late for work, she rushes to the cab rank and still in her nightclub clothes enters a police station where she works as a probationary WPC. A return to the iconoclasm of *Z Cars* is plain to see in *Cops*, both in subject matter and in characterisation. PC Roy Bramell, an old-school copper is not adverse to fitting up the local 'scrotes' aided and abetted by his young hot-headed partner PC Dean Wilshaw. In many senses, similar to Sergeant Twentyman, the granite-faced stoicism of Sergeant Edward Giffen contrasts with the 'sleazy, dishonest, aggressive coke-sniffers who will happily bend rules and plant evidence on people they can't manage to catch by legitimate means' (*The Times*, 20 October 1998). Echoing John Hopkins' comments about the rationale behind his scriptwriting on *Z Cars*, Garnett says of *Cops*:

> As for the police, what are we asking them to do? Are they just neutral upholders of the law? Are they part of a multi-agency

community initiative to heal society's ills? Or are they, when the chips are down, repressive agents of state control? You judge. (Garnett, 1999: 1)

Despite the press reaction to *Cops*, described above and in *The Daily Mirror* as '*Dixon of Dock Green* dragged kicking and cocaine sniffing in to the Nineties' (*Daily Mirror*, 20 October 1998), the series continues to support Clarke's notion of linking police heroes across time. The characters in *Cops* may well appear more overtly flawed than in other contemporary police dramas like *The Bill,* but the police are still represented as human. As in *Z Cars*, officers are seen performing a difficult job in trying circumstances. PC Bramell may well break most of the PACE Codes of Practice in an afternoon, but he still shows care and concern for the innocent, vulnerable people on the Skeetsmoor Estate; WPC Draper ignores an old lady's request to be helped across the road but works hard on a drugs community project. As *The Times* points out:

After just one episode, *Cops* already has the smell of a successful show – provided, of course, it can keep pace with events in real life. In last night's *Panorama*, the reporter Peter Marshall showed us what happened when the West Midlands Police set out to catch its own crooked cops. What we saw made even some of the more flamboyant passages in *Cops* seem a little tame. (*The Times*, 20 October 1998)

As discussed above, the police procedural continually strives to be more 'realistic' than its predecessor, from *Dixon of Dock Green* to *Cops*. Nevertheless, what is of crucial importance is the congruity in the representation of the British bobby on the beat. While the series have altered to reflect and refract current debates about policing, production values have got higher and narratives more complex. The police officer on the beat has remained the heroic, human face of routine law enforcement.

Note

1   Personal communication with John Milne.

Chapter 5

Thief-takers and rule-breakers

Introduction

In recent years, police corruption has received an especially high profile in the media. Cases such as 'Operation Lancet', the three-year inquiry into the Cleveland force and its Superintendent Ray 'Robocop' Mallon, might suggest that police corruption was rife across all forces in England and Wales. *The Daily Telegraph* reported that corruption may have reached 'level 2: the situation which occurs in some Third World Countries' (*The Sunday Telegraph*, 27 September 1998). In March 2002, following the arrest of a Metropolitan police officer for allegedly providing information to known drug dealers, Detective Chief Superintendent Shaun Sawyer, head of the Met's Anti-Corruption Unit, suggested 'Corruption remains a serious threat to police services' (BBC Online, 22 March 2002). But police misconduct is nothing new, as Newburn points out:

> From the earliest days of the Bow Street Runners, through the formation of the New Police in the 1820s, to the vice and porn squad scandals in the 1960s and 1970s, policing in the UK has been punctuated with examples of malpractice and misconduct. (Newburn, 1999: 11)

Thief-taking and rule-breaking have always gone hand in hand, and so it is with fictional representations of the police. From the bending of minor procedural rules to full-blown corruption, rule-breaking is a central theme in representations of the police, particularly in the detective branch. In this chapter, we seek to explore this theme from *The Sweeney*, perhaps the ultimate celebration of the police breaking the rules in order to obtain a conviction, to some of the more predictable crime dramas of the last ten years, where thief-taking and rule-breaking are often just a formula to successful ratings.

Rule-breakers

The battle for right and protection of the public while fighting through ever-increasing bureaucratic red tape has been a constant in police drama since the 1950s. In cinematic representations, the early 1950s signalled a shift away from the celebratory vigilantism of the G-Men films of the 1930s and the proliferation of private detectives throughout the 1940s. Reiner (1981) notes that the central protagonist in many of the police films in the 1950s was 'the tough no-holds barred cop whose unrelenting pursuit of the criminal leads to brutality and illegal methods' (Reiner, 1981: 206). Films such as Orson Welles' *A Touch of Evil* (1958) and Fritz Lang's *The Big Heat* (1953) trod the fine line between endorsing police rule-breaking and attempting to justify it through extraordinary circumstances. Hence in *A Touch of Evil*, idealistic cop Mike Fargas (Charlton Heston) is reduced to framing corrupt police chief Captain Hank Quinlan (Orson Welles) hence the film's tagline: 'The Strangest Vengeance Ever Planned!' Throughout the 1960s and 1970s, Hollywood cop films continued to explore the conflict between crime-solving and rule-abiding. Perhaps the most popular of these was *Dirty Harry* (1971), a continuation of the ends-justifies-the-means theme seen in two previous Don Siegel directed films *Madigan* (1968) and *Coogan's Bluff* (1969). The *Dirty Harry* trailer left the audience in no doubt about Harry Callaghan's methods:

> This is a film about a couple of killers: Harry Callaghan and a homicidal maniac. The one with the badge is Harry...You don't assign him to murder cases. You just turn him loose. (*Dirty Harry*, 1971)

As Reiner comments, *Dirty Harry* represented 'explicit condemnation of the due process requirements laid down by the Supreme Court' (Reiner, 1981: 211). The 'moral economy' (Sparks, 1989: 137) of fictional representations of the police, which includes contemporary police drama on television, is grounded in two things: first, adopting a victim perspective where the harm to society vindicates the utter disregard for due process for the offender; second, the representation of those in power as bureaucratic liberals whose obsession with the minutiae of regulations 'hamstring the work of the street cops by emphasising spit, polish and the rule book...' (Reiner, 1978: 706). Reiner identifies police corruption and rule-breaking in his taxonomy of police drama as 'the vigilante', 'police deviance' and 'deviant police', which account for developments in police deviance in film after the 1970s: Vigilante cops in the film series *Lethal Weapon* and *Die Hard* in the 1980s and 1990s, the bad apple in clean barrel, Reiner's 'deviant police', in *Copland* and *LA Confidential* in 1997, and the reverse: good apple in rotten barrel ('police deviance') in *Serpico* (1973) and *The Untouchables* (1987).

Turning to police drama, it is possible to identify three forms of rule-breaking associated with televisual rule-breaking.

Legitimised or 'noble cause' corruption

This is presented in police drama not as officers breaking the law, but as bending the rules in order to get a conviction. It is undertaken in the pursuit of often altruistic and heroic goals: the apprehension of a known villain, a rogue cop brought to justice, a victim saved, a witness protected. The transgression of rules, however, is not only justified in the manner described above, but it is also limited. Known villains are 'given a pull' and roughed up a bit, search warrants are omitted and the specific orders of senior officers are ignored.

Inherently linked to noble cause corruption is the presentation of the cop as individual. It is not the whole station or even a team that bends the rules, but the individual heroic officer. As Sparks (1992) notes, the law becomes personalised 'where the politics and morality of the enforcement of the law are conflated with the personal moral qualities of the hero' (Sparks, 1992: 134). In their qualitative analysis of crime drama since 1945, Reiner *et al.* (2000a, 2000b) note the increasing portrayal of officers as vigilantes in film. Between 1945 and 1964, they note only 11 per cent of films portraying the police breaking the law which had risen to 23 per cent in films between 1980 and 1991.

Illegitimate rule-breaking

In contrast to the honourable ends pursued by the heroic law-breaking cop, the illegitimate rule-breaker's motives are selfish. Rules are broken for financial gain, power, or respect of colleagues, such actions being motivated by greed and fear. In discussing actual police corruption in Britain, Newburn refers to the 'invitational edges' (Newburn, 1999: 11) of police work, and in particular CID and detective work, where officers, through their daily routines, are brought into close contact with opportunities for dishonesty. In police drama there have been several memorable rotten apples in the police barrel such as DS Don Beech in *The Bill*, who brought about a wholesale clean-up at Sun Hill nick (see Chapter 6). Both *The Vice* and *Between the Lines* had narratives centred around internal police corruption, often at a very high level, while more recently MI5 officer, Tessa Phillips (Jenny Agutter), was found to have falsified information for her own personal financial gain in *Spooks*.

Of course, it is the contrast with the heroic police protagonist that is the primary function of the bad apple with a badge. They are investigated by other officers, hence 'the denunciation of the wrongdoer and a homily from the hero about the revulsion felt for a fellow officer who abused his position of trust' (Clarke, 1983: 48). This is so memorably embodied by George Dixon's comments before arresting another officer for stealing the town hall silver: 'There's nothing worse than a rotten copper. It's the lowest thing that crawls on God's earth'. However, recent police series have blurred the boundaries between these two roles: it is no longer simply a case of the one bad apple in the barrel, as we shall discuss in Chapter 6.

Personal or ethical rule-breaking

It is possible to identify a third type of rule-breaking in the police drama which is not linked to the other two. It concerns the transgression of rules of society, of morals or ethics. This is potentially problematic suggesting a cultural norm: a moral rule of thumb against which to judge police protagonists. The flouting of such norms is, however, celebrated by these series, engendering some notion of anti-heroism. This is perhaps best embodied by Fitz (Robbie Coltrane) in the crime drama *Cracker* about a forensic psychologist working with the police on murder cases. The character of Fitz reverses most of the conventions of a storybook hero. His life is lived to excess: he is a heavy drinker, a gambler, smokes constantly and is overweight. He cheats on his wife with a police officer young enough to be his daughter and, by his own admission, is a failure as a father. In his professional life, he regularly breaks police rules. In one episode, 'Men Should Weep', he throws a rape suspect into a swimming pool to prove that the man cannot swim, thus eliminating him from the police investigation.

Although Fitz displays more flaws than most, there are many other examples of police heroes with weaknesses be it alcohol, women, gambling, violence or all four. From the hard drinking, womanising of Jack Regan in *The Sweeney* and the domestic violence of Bob Steele in *Z Cars*, to the sexual promiscuity of Bob Tate in *Thief-Takers* and Tony Clark in *Between the Lines*, the transgression of these moral boundaries and social norms bestows on the character a human status. Thus while the audience may not approve of Pat Chappel's failure as a father in *The Vice*, such inadequacies coupled with his burning desire to protect vulnerable children may still redeem him and elevate him to hero status. Ultimately Fitz succeeds in securing convictions where more ordinary, less flawed police officers fail but the fact he cannot apply the same razor-sharp analysis of human behaviour to his own life makes him all the more empathetic.

'We're the Sweeney son and we haven't had any dinner'

The first detective drama to fully embrace police corruption, or at least rule-breaking, in the quest for convictions was *The Sweeney*. In his dialectic of police drama, Reiner notes how *The Sweeney* 'was the Dixon image stood on its head' (Reiner, 1994: 24): a move away from the caring approach to policing depicted in *Dixon of Dock Green* and, to some extent, in *Z Cars* towards more of a crime control model:

> To fight crime the police must themselves resort to tactics which appear to mirror those of their foes, using violence and guile for just ends. (Reiner, 1994: 24)

As mentioned in Chapter 3, *The Sweeney* was a product of several in-fluences, both socio-political and media-centric. The late 1960s witnessed the high-profile criminal trials of the Krays, Richardson and Tibbs gangs, while the appointment of Sir Robert Mark as Commissioner of the Metropolitan Police in 1972 on an anti-corruption ticket ensured the maintenance of a high media profile for the police. The 1970s had seen a sharp rise in crime: notifiable offences known to the police rose from 32 per thousand in 1970 to 60 per thousand in 1980 (Hicks and Allen, 1999: 14). The rise in crime was particularly sharp in 1974, with offences recorded as homicide rising from 391 in 1973 to 526 in 1974 (Richards, 1999: 10). As Downes and Morgan (1997: 91) note, the rise in violent crime was taken up by the Conservative Party in their manifesto for the October 1974 election in which they devoted considerable time and space to the issue of law and order. As we saw in Chapter 3, this was also discussed by the Police Federation. On television, representation of the police in Britain in the early 1970s was dominated by two series discussed previously: *Z Cars*, which had shifted a considerable ideological distance from the original iconoclastic drama devised by John McGrath and Ian Kennedy-Martin, and the restful world of *Dixon of Dock Green*, which was still occupying early Saturday evenings. Clarke (1986) points out that attempts had been made to move police drama forward with *Special Branch* (1969–74, Thames Television), *Fraud Squad* (1969–70) and the *Z Cars* spin-off *Softly Softly* (1966–76). But the key to understanding the impetus for the emergence of *The Sweeney* lies in the development of the genre in the United States, on the big and small screen.

In Hollywood, fictional representations of cops had taken a violent turn in the 1970s with the Clint Eastwood vehicles *Dirty Harry* (1971), *Magnum Force* (1973) and later *The Enforcer* (1976), and *The French Connection* (1971). Reiner comments that '...the ultimate weight of the cycle [of cop films in the 1970s] was politically reactionary, supporting hard-line "law and order" policies' (Reiner, 1981: 209). Similarly, Clarke (1987) notes the American police procedural on television, embodied in series like *Dragnet*, were replaced by a 'more action-oriented formula with plenty of car chases, fights and shootings' (Clarke, 1987: 37). The popularity with US audiences of series like *Kojak* and *Starsky and Hutch* were replicated in the UK when the BBC began importing the shows. Against their slick quick American counterparts, *Dixon* and *Z Cars* appeared slow and ponderous, lumbering through dense procedural detail: 'the series which had dominated British TV schedules suddenly became anachronistic, a nostalgic legacy of days gone by' (Clarke, 1983: 47). Although it was the BBC that successfully screened the American cop shows, it was ITV that chose to make a British version of the 'rough, tough, kick 'em in the teeth crime series' (Reiner, 1994: 24).

Thames Television had set up Euston Films at the beginning of the 1970s with a remit for producing television and film drama. One of its early projects was a series of 90-minute films designed for television. There were six *Armchair Cinemas* made, one of which, *Regan*,[1] had received high audience ratings[2] and was eventually sold to 47 countries (www.thesweeney.com/swhistor.htm). As a result, 13 one-hour programmes were made incorporating the core elements of *Regan* but the name was changed to *The Sweeney*, the nickname for The Met's Flying Squad.[3] Writers were given a strict set of guidelines to follow which included a screen time of 48 minutes 40 seconds, a pre-title sequence of 3 minutes and three acts of between 8 and 19 minutes. The character of Jack Regan (played by the late John Thaw) was to appear in every episode.

The centrality of Regan to *The Sweeney* is seen as crucial by several commentators on the series. Hurd (1981) talks of the 'centred biography' of the series, in which the two other principal characters, Regan's sidekick DS George Carter (Dennis Waterman) and Flying Squad boss Chief Inspector Frank Haskins (Garfield Morgan), exist in relation to Regan. Regan is focused as 'the tough individualistic, freebooting cop' (Hurd,

1981: 61), similar to the 'lone wolf cop' in Reiner's (2000b) analysis, a vigilante in the vein of 1970s US cops like Theo Kojak, Popeye Doyle and 'Dirty' Harry Callahan:

> Only the streetwise cop, understanding the vicious nature of criminals, can deal effectively with them, defying the restraints posed by legal or departmental rules and regulations. (Reiner, 2000b: 155)

However, Clarke (1986) suggests that the constraints of British police drama heritage make Regan a diluted version of the likes of Dirty Harry, hence he is 'moderately permissive but heterosexual. He is a moderately heavy drinker but not an alcoholic'. His rule-breaking too is confined to what is necessary to catch the villain, hence the legal shackles are broken open to enable justice to be done. As Hurd comments: 'Justice and law are inviolable, given, not to be confused with the frequently flawed mechanisms by which they are obtained' (Hurd, 1981: 66).

The Sweeney presented a form of legitimised corruption in which the ruthless pursuit of the villain may well entail 'the short cutting of legal niceties' (Hurd, 1981: 66). For Regan to absolve himself of the responsibilities of due process accorded to suspects by other law enforcement agencies, crime in *The Sweeney* is represented as a faceless evil perpetrated by 'villains who must be fought and stamped out, and can only be combatted successfully by police officers who are equally ruthless' (Reiner, 1994: 24). Crime is no longer portrayed as a social ill of the community as depicted in *Z Cars*, but a battle taking place in the urban jungle of London, where violence 'is perceived as a problem but not problematic' (Hurd, 1976: 49).

Hurd further suggests that *The Sweeney* presents the fight against crime in a literal sense both explicitly (Regan to Haskins – 'Don't you realise it's a war out there?') and implicitly: 'the planning and counter-planning in each camp, the military-style conduct of police and criminals, manoeuvuring for tactical and strategic advantage, and the final set-piece battle...' (Hurd, 1976: 49). In this context, the transgression of normal police boundaries is celebrated, ultimately in the apprehension, or possibly death, of the villain. All is fair in love and war. The moment of apprehension itself signifies the conviction of the criminal, for in *The Sweeney* 'it is not in the courts that convictions are obtained but in the face-to-face world of police and villains' (Hurd, 1981: 57).

A second legitimising source for rule-breaking in *The Sweeney* is the depiction of bureaucracy embodied by Haskins as 'the man upstairs' who must censure Regan 'for his quasi-criminal violence and his anarchic posturing' (Drummond, 1976: 25). The official procedures appear as red tape, constricting Regan's heroic attempts to shield the public from the growing menace of crime. Senior officers are portrayed as colluding 'with the politicians and lawyers who force the police to operate with one hand tied behind their backs by due process of law restrictions' (Reiner, 1994: 24). This is best summed up by Regan's oft-quoted monologue in 'Abduction':

> 'I sometimes hate this bastard place. It's a bloody holiday camp for thieves and weirdos, all the rubbish. You age prematurely trying to sort some of them out. Try and protect the public and all they do is call you 'fascist'. You nail a villain and some ponced up, pinstriped Hampstead barrister screws it up like an old fag packet on a point of procedure and then pops off for a game of squash and a glass of Madeira. He's taking home thirty grand a year, and we can just about afford ten days in Eastbourne and a second-hand car. No, it's all bloody wrong my son.'

Clarke observed in 1983 that '…the cluster of ideological values that characterised the police… has remained remarkably untouched to the present day' (Clarke, 1983: 48). This was as true in 1974 when Regan first appeared as it is to police dramas in the twenty-first century. Notwithstanding his abrasive, recusant stance, Regan still stood for many of the core Dixonian values championed twenty years earlier. Uncorrupted, unwavering and undaunted, he protects the public, keeping the streets clean, albeit supplanting the quiet word in the ear of the dodgy street trader with a punch in the face of the hooded, armed villain.

As Tulloch (1990) points out, *The Sweeney* was very much of its time. As we have seen, the rise in violent crime and the influence of American cop shows demanded a change in direction for the police show. The series was not simply a faithful representation of thief-taking in 1970s London but was a combination of the audience's partial knowledge of policing, previous police shows and the conditions of production. This latter issue should not be underestimated. Drummond (1976) notes a number of important production restrictions on authenticity for the producers of *The Sweeney*. These include no locations further than one hour's drive from Hammersmith; no more than three minutes night shooting; at least ten minutes of each episode to be situated within the studio mock-up of Scotland Yard. Hence the series refracted rather than reflected police issues at the time, working in conjunction with audience knowledge, constraints of production and public debates about policing (Clarke, 1986). Whereas *The Sweeney* broke the mould with its portrayal of the rule-breaking cop, the contemporary thief-taking drama is often less ambitious.

Rule-breaking, but not always ground-breaking

Throughout the 1990s, crime drama series continued to depict the close relationship between thief-taking and rule-breaking. With the honourable exceptions of *Between the Lines* and *The Vice*, these police shows brought very little that was new to the fictional representation of the police. Their role in the development of the police detective drama formula is worthy of discussion. Here, we outline the structure and common themes evident in *The Vice*, *Liverpool 1, Burnside* and *Thief-Takers*.

The Vice

Carlton Television's *The Vice* was first broadcast in January 1999 and has run for three series. As the title suggests, the programme focused on the London Metropolitan Police's Vice Squad. Based in the sleazy world of illegal drinking clubs, prostitution, pornography and drugs, the principal character of the series is Detective Inspector Pat Chappel (Ken Stott), a forty-something, recently divorced copper described by Bond (1999) as 'the inevitably maverick vice-squad officer obsessed with his work and curiously sympathetic to some of its victims'. Two other officers flank him: Detective Sergeant Joe Robinson (David Harewood), a black family-man officer who finds that his work increasingly conflicts with his home life; and Detective Constable Cheryl Hutchins (Anna Chancellor and later Caroline Catz), a loyal officer who shares Chappel's desire to do right, but not always his methods. Series one and the early part of series two also featured rookie vice-squad officer Dougie (Mark Chapman) a young, inexperienced 'loose cannon' whose impetuousity leads first to his dismissal, followed by his 'crossing the line' to work for a vice baron, and finally to his execution by a London gang when it is discovered that he has been acting as Chappel's informant.

Liverpool 1

Like *The Vice*, *Liverpool 1* centred on vice squad work, this time at Liverpool's Bridewell police station. The Yorkshire Television production ran for two six-part series, beginning in September 1998. The series is based around a team of five officers, but follows the progress of two in particular. Detective Sergeant Isobel De Pauli (Samantha Janus), recently transferred from the Met's Club and Vice Unit, and Detective Sergeant

Mark Callaghan ('Cally' played by Mark Womack). De Pauli and Cally form one of two teams both overseen by Detective Inspector Howard Jones (Tom Georgeson, who played Harry Naylor in *Between the Lines*). De Pauli has a psychology degree, is loyal to her colleagues and also self-reliant. Her intellectualism is contrasted with Cally, whom Yorkshire Television's press release describes as '…an animal of instinct and extremes: sex, drinks, fights – he never does things by halves, but he's also shrewd, committed to his work and never lets playing hard get in the way' (www.liverpool1.merseyworld.com).

The series returns us to familiar CID territory – drugs, prostitution, murder and child abuse. However, running through the programme is the central theme of family: Callaghan's three other brothers and one sister are all developed in the series, and there is a focus on the aftermath of crimes on victims' families: the bereaved father, the abused daughter and so on. Also there is the inevitable sexual tension between the leading characters: the 'will-they-won't-they?' factor, reminiscent of Mulder and Scully in *The X Files*.

Burnside

Burnside was a spin off from *The Bill*, albeit more than ten years after Frank Burnside (Chris Ellison) first appeared in the popular police procedural. It ran for three two-part stories in the summer of 2000. Detective Inspector Burnside was head of a team of four officers as part of the National Crime Squad. 'The British FBI' he informs his colleagues.[4] The breathless press release from Pearson Television explained that the NCS:

> …tackles organised crime in Britain and abroad – the biggest villains, the grandest scams, the toughest targets. Burnside's unit delves into the darker side of crime and becomes involved in the murky world of illegal firearms, gang warfare, and goes on the trail of a serial killer. (www.burnside.co.uk)

Like *Liverpool 1*, the four officers in Burnside's team form two partnerships. The first consisted of Detective Constables Moss and Gibson. However much more central to the series, and typically supporting Burnside, were Detective Sergeant Dave Summers and Detective Constable Sam Philips. The series was 'surprisingly (and somewhat implausibly) politically correct' (Hoggart, 2000: 23) with a gay mixed race officer in Summers said to be 'suave, sophisticated and at the cutting edge of intelligent policing' (www.burnside.co.uk/characters) and an attractive, acerbic, ambitious young female detective in Philips. The series followed the structure of other post modern crime drama in its representation of dirty police work, legitimised rule-bending, loyalty to the team, and the heroic – at times anti-heroic – fight against crime. Burnside's age and old-school policing methods were shown to get results: nicking villains is in Burnside's blood and he cannot retire while there are 'scumbags' walking the streets. The narrative was structured in such a way that it is Burnside who had to save the day, a denouement underscored by peripheral characters making comments along the way like 'you better pray Burnside finds him'.

Thief-Takers

First broadcast in 1995, *Thief-Takers* was a Carlton Television police drama that ran for three series. It differed slightly from the other series discussed so far in that it focused on a much larger team rather than the teams of three or four in similar dramas. *Thief-Takers* was in many respects an update of *The Sweeney*, concerned as it was with the London Metropolitan Police's Flying Squad. A team of seven was led by the young and ambitious DI Charlie Scott (Reece Dinsdale); principal characters include DC's Alan Oxford, Bob 'Bingo' Tate and Grace Harris. Like *The Sweeney* before it, *Thief-Takers* centred on serious and organised crime, in particular robbery, drug dealing and murder. As the video box blurb notes:

> The elite band of officers…find themselves up against some of the underworld's meanest and toughest villains who are prepared to go to all lengths to get their hands on the prize, targeting banks, building societies, jewellers, security vans and anything that offers big rewards. (*Thief-Takers*: The Complete Series One, Pearson Television)

Crime and criminals

These detective series tend to portray offenders as greedy, depraved and, very often, mentally disordered. This is consistent with the findings of Reiner *et al.* (2000a) who suggest that the criminal has been consistently portrayed unsympathetically in fiction since 1945, and as 'purely evil and enjoying their offending' (Reiner *et al.* 2000a: 20) in 85 per cent of their sample of crime fiction since 1980. The criminal, however, has moved on from the two-dimensional, tooled-up 'toe-rag' of *The Sweeney* and has acquired a semblance of psychological depth. This development of the fictional offender owes much to *Cracker* (1993–96) and *Prime Suspect* (1991–95), both of which introduced characters of greater cognitive complexity, with darker motives and an ability to elude the law. In *Burnside* the cast of criminals included a right-wing extremist driven to kidnapping his business partner's child, a serial killer with acute sexual problems and a weak suspect with a liking for underage girls. In *The Vice*, children are lured away from a residential home into prostitution by a man from a children's home who is himself afraid of the dark; a nameless gangster bullies one of his call girls hitting her and bribing her with drugs. While in *Thief-Takers* and *Liverpool 1*, heads of organised crime gangs put money and power ahead of family and loved ones.

Sparks (1992) points out that the criminal must exhibit equally exceptional traits as the police hero, 'their monstrous character should both oppose and justify the hero's deeds' (Sparks, 1992: 141). Such representations not only allow for law enforcers to shine against the murky nefariousness of the criminal, but enables overt, brusque condemnation of offenders. In Burnside it is perhaps more straightforward: the villains that he pursues are 'crazy psychos', 'slags' and 'bastards', echoing the words of his spiritual ancestor in police drama, Jack Regan.

Condemnation of the criminal is underscored by these series' emphasis on the victims, who are typically defenceless, vulnerable people. The excesses of the criminal are shown to have knock-on effects on the naive and afraid: children, families and the elderly. Many stories involve children: who go missing, turn up dead or in prostitution. In *The Vice*, there is a voyeuristic depiction of a seamy world which has an appeal similar to the fictional representations of the serial killer: the darkest side of human nature, excessive, hedonistic, violent. Yet *The Vice* takes on a dual role in providing the thrills while simultaneously censuring them. Both these elements are present in the title sequence: a scantily clad woman moves in slow motion while violent scenes unfold around her and a parallel screen shows a police arrest. There are stories involving predatory sex offenders and abusive fathers. In *Liverpool 1* this echoes the central theme of family running through the series and this perhaps is the feature that sets it apart from the others. There is an attempt to balance the representation of organised violent crime with an exploration of family relationships. This aspect, coupled with its location in Merseyside, render it possible to draw similarities with the early *Z Cars* series. Problems within families and social issues connected with drugs and poverty replicate some of the 1960s series' essential themes. However, in spirit, it is more reminiscent of the work of Jimmy McGovern and of *Cracker* in particular. Its treatment of family, religion, sex and death add further dimensions to crime and law enforcement, suggesting that crime is motivated by more complex emotions than good old-fashioned greed, gratification or revenge.

The crimes focused on by these series are organised, serious crime: armed robbery, drug gangs, serial killers, terrorists and paedophiles. Notwithstanding the attempt at psychological development of the criminal, villains still possess many of the well-worn characteristics of the London gangster left over from *The Sweeney* and seen in recent spin-offs like *Lock, Stock and Two Smoking Barrels*[5] (1998): sharp suited, violent miscreants strutting around with a secreted sawn-off ready for pump action. There is an alternation between the labyrinthine netherworld where crimes are committed: locations such as railway lines, canals, waste ground, sex shops and disused warehouses, and the places where the villains spend their ill-gotten gains: boats, nightclubs, restaurants and so on. This is perhaps best illustrated by the big country house (garishly decorated of course) owned by the head of the crime gang: the arch-criminal, softly spoken, whose penchant for violence remains visible below the surface. The constant threat of danger is a repetitive theme, reminding the audience of the risk that the heroic law enforcer undertakes in his quest to apprehend the villain and protect the public. Pat Chappel, Cally, Burnside, Bingo and the others generally emerge victorious, but the victory can often be a Pyrrhic one, as is so often the case with Chappel whose integrity and personal relationships are further corroded and tainted, just like those of the victims he seeks to protect.

All of the series mentioned are based in big cities: three in London, one in Liverpool, a fact emphasised visually with both opening and ending credit sequences based around city locations, and individual episodes punctuated by aerial shots at night of the city. Crime often takes place at recognisable London landmarks: Heathrow, Embankment and Battersea Power Station among others. As Sparks notes:

> The sheer size of the city and its geographical and social segmentation, its scale as a container of power and wealth, its polyglot diversity and ethnic divisions make it a place for inward exploration. (Sparks, 1992: 126)

In *Liverpool 1*, the city is central to the series, as Colin McKeown the producer of the series commented: 'With these scripts there is a real sense of the place and culture. *Liverpool 1* is different in that the city is a character, just as Edinburgh and Glasgow were in *Taggart*' (www.liverpool1.merseyworld.com).

Portrayal of the police

As we have seen earlier, the representation of the bobby on the beat, from *Dixon* to *Cops*, is essentially a favourable, somewhat heroic one. Research into broader depictions of law enforcement (Clarke, 1983, 1986; Hurd, 1981; Laing, 1991; Leishman, 1995; Mason, 1992; Mawby, 1997a, 1997b, 1998a, 1998b; Reiner, 1981, 1991, 1994, 2000a, 2000b; Robards, 1985; Sparks, 1989, 1992) also confirm that the police officer is attributed heroic status. The modern crime drama is no exception. Each protagonist battles to protect the public against crime, in the face of bureaucracy, citizen apathy and outright hostility. The officers here eat, drink and sleep police work at considerable personal cost to themselves. Pat Chappel in *The Vice* is a single man with a failed marriage and teetering on the verge of burn-out. He is a heavy drinker, who is regularly seen crashing out drunk on late-night whisky. His flat is an unsightly mess and he sometimes sleeps in his clothes. Frank Burnside is divorced and portrayed as a loner, so too is Cally in *Liverpool 1*. In *Thief-Takers*, Bob Tate is divorced with a string of casual sexual relationships including one with an informant, while DC Helen Ash's marriage is suffering from her all-consuming career, a familiar storyline echoed in *Liverpool 1* with De Pauli's eventual separation from her partner. One can point to similarities with Jane Tennison (Helen Mirren) in *Prime Suspect*, and more recently with DC Jack Mowbray (Ross Kemp) in *Without Motive*, a series created by veteran *Between the Lines* writer Rob Heyland.

The officers in these series are further developed as heroes and heroines through their constant battle with bureaucracy and red tape. In 'Home Is the Place', Pat Chappel picks up a girl who has run away from a childrens' home in Sheffield. After trying to find her a place in another home and getting nowhere he screams at the office, 'Am I the only one who is interested in this?' In this battle, official by-the-book investigation is seen by the police hero and heroine as providing protection for the villain. In order to maintain audience support for this perspective, authority is embodied in inflexible, out-of-touch management. In *Burnside* this is depicted through an ongoing conflict between Burnside's intuitive feel for a villain's collar and Superintendent Brian Lees's desire to follow proper procedure. This tension is further exacerbated by Burnside's past:

> 'This is exactly why I didn't want you here. You work for Frank Burnside and no one else. You don't care about anybody else as long as you get a result. You should have been hitting golf balls in The Algarve years ago.'

The bureaucrats are there to be rebelled against: otherwise their desk-bound, managerialist dogma will restrict the protagonist's options and reduce them to something more ordinary. Their consequent opposing stance is celebrated as it inevitably leads to the apprehension of the criminal. Hurd (1981) identifies this conflict as 'professional versus organization':

> ...the self-sufficient group, functioning without the organisational apparatus of a large scale bureaucratic institution and resenting interference... (Hurd, 1981: 67)

In *The Vice*, Inspector Chappel is very much the knight in tarnished armour, saving the underprivileged and vulnerable from greedy, violent pimps, drug barons and gangster overlords; in *Thief-Takers*, Charlie and his team resplendent in flak jackets and baseball caps risk taking a bullet to prevent a bank raid or the importation of huge amounts of crack cocaine.

The emerging theme from these programmes, inherently linked with traditional notions of heroism and resistance to authority, is the prevalence of anti-heroism. This is perhaps most memorably embodied in the hard-drinking, compulsive gambling criminal psychologist Fitz in *Cracker*. The flaws in the protagonist may be physical: in *The Vice* Chappel is not conventionally attractive – he is scruffy, unkempt, in poor physical shape and drinks and smokes too much. The flaws may also be moral: Bob Tate's serial womanising in *Thief-Takers*, Cally's brother losing a leg while acting as an informant for Cally in *Liverpool 1*. Cally's extended family and relationships with chief villain Sullivan also border on collusion in places. We learn of his wealthy background, the 'working-class hero' with an upper-middle-class bank balance, and we see his interconnections with his brothers – the priest, the drug-addicted informant, the naive entrepreneur and all their partners and offspring. Cally, of course, remains the quintessential loner, the solo cop who battles for right according to a personal code that transcends the procedural manual.

Perhaps more entertaining is the portrayal of Frank Burnside, who cannot escape his fictional roots, as he owes most of his character to Jack Regan, a cynical hardened thief-taker who devotes his waking hours to protecting his manor. In the pre-title sequence of the first episode, 'Back with a Vengeance', an off-duty Burnside apprehends an armed robber on a cross-Channel ferry with the obligatory 'you're nicked'. For Burnside, like Regan, the ends justify the means – search warrants can wait, but cleaning 'scum' off the streets cannot. Yet it is precisely these aspects of

Burnside's character that are celebrated by the series – 'A shameless old cliche' (Hoggart, 2000: 23), the series recognises this issue and places it centre stage. Five minutes into episode one, DC Philips comments 'he's a dinosaur…we're modern, streamlined, low profile – no place for him here' but the all-knowing Burnside mixes his traditional policing methods ('where's your warrant?' 'It's in the post') with a postmodern ironic awareness of his surroundings.

Burnside gains further empathy from the audience with his self-deprecation: when Philips asks why he does not like her, he replies: 'I'm a sexist bigot, I don't have to give you a reason'. This is tempered with his ability to reinvent himself – he is shown to be technology-literate, working with digital cameras, laptops and other information-age gadgetry, the new iconography of the police drama. His machismo is reserved for the criminal: there is no overt sexism in his treatment of Philips ('she's the daughter I never had'), nor homophobia in his dealings with Summers. Indeed this is in contrast to the attitude of other officers: Burnside is accused of sleeping with Philips and there is an allusion to Summers getting beaten up at his old police station because of his sexual orientation. Perhaps most interestingly, Burnside shows an awareness of the public perception of the police. Several times he refers to how the media would report the cases they are working on: 'We've gotta stop this bastard before he's got a dedicated website and the tabloids are screaming "Perv Killer Makes Mockery of Old Bill" '(in 'Exposed').

While it is true to say that much police drama during the 1990s was formulaic and predictable, one series had a much bigger impact. *Between the Lines*, which won 'Best Drama Series' at the BAFTAs in 1993, represented a departure from the relationship between rule-breakers and thief-takers depicted thus far.

The thin blurred line

Between the Lines was first broadcast in 1992 and was created by John Wilsher, a veteran scriptwriter for *The Bill*. The series was produced by Tony Garnett, who had previously worked on other police procedurals like *Z Cars* and *Dixon of Dock Green* and later produced *Cops*. It ran for two very successful series and a not so successful third one that turned the show from 'the classiest, sharpest, most convincing police drama ever produced in this country into a conspiracy-thon' (White, 1994). The programme shifted the focus of crime to within the police force, centring on the CIB, a fictional police Complaints Investigation Bureau. It is arguable that this was a reflection of policing at the time with highly publicised cases of police mismanagement and corruption, such as the miscarriages of justice cases of the Guildford Four and the Birmingham Six. Furthermore, as Leishman puts it, *Between the Lines* was among the first police series to explore 'not only policing on the streets, but also policing from the suites' (Leishman, 1995: 148).

After receiving his promotion, successful, ambitious and handsome police officer Detective Superintendent Tony Clark (Neil Pearson) reluctantly accepts a post to CIB, a unit dedicated to sorting out bent coppers. His team consists of Detective Inspector Harry Naylor (Tom Georgeson), an old-school, salt-of-the-earth copper, who knows the villain on the street and is both loyal to the job and his dying wife, and Detective Sergeant Maureen (Mo) Connell (Siobhan Redmond) – a foil to the male bonding of Clark and Naylor, an officer whose sexual orientation and politics are brought to the fore in several episodes. The team are answerable to John Deakin (Tony Doyle), a hardened senior officer whose political machinations in government and business provide the climax to the series' running theme of corruption and conspiracy.

Between the Lines dealt with real 1990s policing problems: public order, housing estates awash with drugs and guns, racism both inside and outside of the force, and sexual politics. The series smudged the thin blue line between criminal deviance and law enforcement, allowing for an exploration of police corruption at all levels as well as in government. Power struggles, tenebrious dealings and flexible ethics formed the central core of the programme.

Although one might consider a series dealing with police corruption to be inherently critical of the police, the series simply drew a line, albeit a blurred one, between the transgressor of police rules and the heroic cop personified in Clark. The rotten cop in the barrel was not always entirely rotten. The murky areas of policing and the portrayal of the police as under stress and doing a difficult job led to a blurring between good and evil, 'between the lines' of the title. Therefore we see Clark investigating 'a copper who gets results': the most successful CID officer in the Met guilty of taking a bribe from a con in 'The Great Detective'; an undercover officer who has infiltrated a racist skinhead group ('New Order') and conspiracy in secret service cover-ups and big business in 'Big Boys' Rules'.

One result of this obfuscation is to continue the 'linking of police heroes across time' (Clarke, 1986: 266), both in the portrayal of officers as human with frailties and flaws which cause them to be corrupt and in the heroic nature of those who investigate their corrupt colleagues. *Between the Lines* has three principal heroes but Tony Clark is firmly the protagonist in the series. The title sequence places him at the centre of the action, a turning head shot while scenes from episodes of the whole series play out behind him. The opening episode is telling in its introduction of Clark to the audience. It is worth briefly describing 'Private Enterprise' as it establishes for the audience Clark's dominant characteristics. The episode opens with Clark at his leaving party taking congratulations on his promotion, drinking, smoking, joshing with the lads. He leaves with young WPC Jenny Dean and, having had sex with her in his car, drives home to his wife. Further scenes of him drinking and smoking punctuate the episode. Clark is also shown standing up for himself, being ambitious and being no respecter of authority. In his chat with Commander Huxtable and Chief Superintendent John Deakin, they comment how Clark 'played a blinder' at his promotions board. Ultimately Clark succeeds in the task set him by his superiors: he brings the corrupt senior officer to justice and wins his promotion. He also makes enemies, ignores orders and conflicts with senior officers: characteristics that are likely to extend his appeal.

However heroic, Clark is fundamentally flawed, a blurred character. He is a thief-taker, but is also a liar – cheating on his wife and various other women and he is shown to be a rule-breaker in his investigations. Nevertheless, the rule-breaking by Clark is shown as justified – legitimate rule-breaking as pioneered by *The Sweeney* forms a central part of Clark's strategy. Although usually successful, and notwithstanding the oppositional discourse proffered by Maureen Connell, mistakes and misjudgements in Clark's personal life counter the heroics in his professional life: his marriage, which is initially in difficulty, ends in divorce. He subsequently makes a fool of himself with the older, wiser and more powerful Angela Berridge (Francesca Annis): the antithesis of naive and malleable Jenny Dean from series one. The rule-breaking here then is not always clear. On the one hand we are presented with routine police corruption, depicted as unacceptable, yet on the other we have Clark's rule-breaking: legitimated as the only way to get results. This is further justified in the contrast of Clark's superiors – in particular Graves and Sullivan. Sullivan is the out of touch Commander who wants things done by the book, while Graves is Clark's rule-abiding, desk-bound line manager. Both are seen as dull, grey and lacking compared with the racy, sexy and opportunistic Clark. However, even the apparently squeaky clean Sullivan turns out to be a rule-breaker. In one episode, Clark uses his knowledge of Sullivan's past misdemeanour to have Harry Naylor's disciplinary charge reduced ('What's the Strength of This?'). This act of 'noble cause' rule-breaking increases rather diminishes Clark's heroic status.

Conclusion

Since *The Sweeney*, rule-breaking has been portrayed as inextricably linked with crime-solving in detective drama. As Harry comments in an episode of *Between the Lines*:

> 'You can't expect people who do the rough stuff to stay virgins…You show me one Mr bloody Squeeky Clean with half the results he's got and I'll eat your PACE manual darlin'. (From 'The Great Detective')

However, while *The Sweeney* and its generally less inventive drama-by-numbers successors portray a clear distinction between the necessity of legitimate rule-breaking and the unacceptability of self-satisfying police corruption, *Between the Lines* blurs these boundaries. The moral decline of more recent police heroes like Pat Chappel in *The Vice* signal a movement towards a less certain division between traditional notions of good and evil. Indeed, at the end of series three, Chappel fitted up the demonic detective played by Tim Piggot-Smith on a rape charge, reminiscent of Charlton Heston's cop in *A Touch of Evil*. While that may have been the strangest vengeance ever planned in 1958, in the contemporary TV copland, it is maybe less out of place.

Notes

1 Broadcast on the ITV network on 4 June 1974.
2 Seven million, rank numbered three that week in the BARB ratings (www.thesweeney.com/epascii.txt).
3 The shortened Cockney rhyming slang, Sweeney Todd – Flying Squad.
4 The National Crime Squad has featured in several recent police dramas including the BBC's *NCS* and *The Whistle Blower*.
5 These include *Love, Honour and Obey, Gangster Number One, Rancid Aluminium, Essex Boys* (all 2000) and *Sexy Beast* (2001).

Chapter 6

The changing contours of TV copland

Introduction

As noted in Chapter 3, from as far back as the 1850s, two public images of the police have predominated – the bobby and the detective – and, as Chapters 4 and 5 have suggested, these have continued to represent the mainstay characters of TV crime drama, albeit with differing degrees of emphasis over time along a 'caring-controlling' continuum (Reiner, 1994). Ellis Cashmore observed that, 'While moods and tastes have shifted over the decades, crime drama has been television's *terra firma*' (1994: 155), accounting for something like a quarter of all programming time, attracting consistently high ratings, commanding considerable audience loyalty, with individual series often enjoying greater longevity than many popular soap operas. The variety of styles and forms of crime drama has derived in large measure from classic detective fiction, featuring as their heroes such famous amateur or consulting detectives as Agatha Christie's Hercule Poirot and Miss Marple, Dorothy L. Sayer's Lord Peter Wimsey and, of course, Sir Arthur Conan Doyle's Sherlock Holmes, each of whom constitutes an example of what Reiner memorably dubbed 'the eccentric hero with super-charged neurons' (2000b: 153). A number of professional police characters have also made the transition from paperback to small screen, ranging from the elite and exceptional, like Ngaio Marsh's Alleyn, P. D. James's Dalgliesh and Colin Dexter's Morse, to the more downbeat and dogged like R. D. Wingfield's Denton DI Jack Frost and Ian Rankin's Edinburgh based Rebus. The 'private eye' has also crossed media and Atlantic, from the pages of the likes of Raymond Chandler and Dashiell Hammett, through the airwaves and *films noirs* of the 1940s, and into a myriad of made-for-TV manifestations from the early 1950s onwards. Somewhere in the late 1950s/early 1960s, the TV cop show's rise intersected with the Western's demise as the dominant dramatic setting for the modern mass-media morality play. As Robards put it:

> The police show is television's heroic genre, and the arbitration of right and wrong for society has become the function of the television cop. (1985: 24)

In the earliest years, TV copland was indeed a place of moral certainty and of the assured restoration of peace and order, the bell or siren of the speeding police patrol car providing for audiences the same sort of reassurance of a satisfactory outcome as had the bugle and horse hooves of the advancing 7th Cavalry in countless conventional Westerns, the urban policeman's badge updating the frontier sheriff's silver star. However, as Cashmore suggests, it has taken some forty years for television's 'heroic genre' to mature and move beyond the 'flat parables of good and evil [which] dominated North American and British crime drama until the 1990s' (1994: 155). For it was during that decade that the topography of TV copland underwent some significant changes, changes that reflect the cultural salience and political resonance throughout the 1980s and 1990s of what Brunsdon (2000: 197–200) identifies as three relevant and related 'discursive contexts', which affected real-life policing as much as its fictional representations. First there was the ascendancy of an increasingly punitive political agenda on law and order, second the phenomenon of privatisation and a concomitant 'privileging' of private enterprise and, third, the discourse of equal opportunities, and in particular its implications for the occupational culture of the police. To these we must also add a fourth element, a context which we have alluded to in earlier chapters, namely the recognition that we live in a 'risk society' (Beck, 1992), characterised by 'ambient insecurity' (Bauman, 1998), and in which 'our engagement with crime and punishment is inherently ambiguous' (Sparks, 2000: 210). The contours of contemporary copland television texts and the heroes who inhabit them have been shaped in interesting ways by these various influences, as we hope to demonstrate, through discussion of what we term the 'hybrid' police procedural. We then give consideration to televisual representations of police culture and diversity and how these have shifted in the last decade or so. Finally, through reflection on Robert Reiner's (1994; 2000b) influential frameworks, our own earlier work (Mason, 1992; Leishman, 1995) and the insightful accounts of others, notably Brunsdon (2000) and Green (2000), we endeavour to extend and update Reiner's earlier dialectical progression model of the British police procedural as a means of highlighting how the contours of TV copland have changed.

No more heroes?

Police and detective heroes in literary, film and TV forms, have assumed various guises in the course of crime drama history. Setting to one side the classic sleuth and private eye models, Reiner's comprehensive typology of the law enforcement story (Reiner, 2000b: 149–60), focuses mainly on the public police, many of the classic British examples having had as their heroes the plods and patrol cops that we examined in Chapter 4, and the thief-takers and rule-breakers of Chapter 5. However, it should be noted that some types of public police narrative identified by Reiner are more readily associated with star-driven Hollywood movies, rather than the small screen, as is suggested in Table 6.1.

We would argue, however, that – on British TV at least – it is possible to identify from the early 1990s the emergence of a new species of police drama that is perhaps principally defined by what it is not. We will call this the hybrid police procedural, for the story type does not fit neatly into Reiner's taxonomy, although some elements of those ideal-type narratives are certainly present. These hybrids are neither police procedurals nor community police dramas in the tradition of 1960s *Dixon* or 1980s *The Bill*, as their focus is generally more specialised. Typically the heroes are small teams of officers often operating in packs of three or four,

Table 6.1 Typology of police drama narratives

Story type	Hero type	Example
Police procedural	Routine cop	*Z Cars*
Vigilante	Lone-wolf cop	*Dirty Harry*
Civil rights	Dedicated legalistic cop	*Mississippi Burning*
Undercover cop	Skilful 'blender'	*I.D.*
Police deviance	Honest loner cop	*Serpico*
Deviant police	Rogue cop/Freudian fuzz	*Internal Affairs*
Let 'em have it	Elite gangbusters	*The Sweeney*
Fort Apache	Team of routine cops	*Cops*
Police community	Routine patrol cops	*The Bill*
Community police	Routine patrol bobby	*Dixon of Dock Green*

Adapted from Reiner (2000b: 150–2).

rather than the lone-wolf cop that Reiner discusses in relation to his 'vigilante' cop show. In some respects they are similar to the elite gangbusters of his 'let 'em have it' strand, although cracking organised crime is not necessarily the primary plotline. The centrality of the tight-knit, though by no means homogeneous, team in the hybrid procedural represents, in many senses, a fusion of all three types of relationship for TV police heroes identified by Sparks (1992), namely either one of a pair, leader or senior officer, or loner at odds with authority.

While there are clearly echoes of police deviance tales like *LA Confidential* (1997) and *Copland* (1997) the story of our hybrid police procedural is not principally about the 'good apple in the rotten barrel' nor the 'bad apple in the clean barrel' (Reiner, 2000b: 156–7). Having said that, the hybrid procedural tends to be populated with a more than usual representation of deviant police, the villain-in-chief often taking the form of a 'demonic detective', someone who wields considerable influence inside both the police world and the underworld – a person of sub-terranean values. What we would suggest that this strand of police drama tends to present is more of an 'apple crumble' effect in which, under a crumbling façade of police propriety, good apples and bad apples coexist in a mix, and are not always easily distinguishable one from another.

Generally speaking, the hybrid procedural format is a one-hour drama series, focused on a specialist team dealing with serious crimes in an urban setting which is usually detached from any real sense of com-munity. Production values are high, often being shot on film in the 'slickly edited, but naturalistic style' that Brunsdon terms 'grubby realism' (2000: 212). Another common feature is that in addition to episode-specific stories, there is a running and ultimately enveloping subplot, which does not necessarily result in a clear-cut resolution of order and moral dilemmas as, in the main, is the case with the plot structures of Reiner's ideal types. We would identify as hybrids some of the more recent 'thief-taker rule-breaker' dramas, singling out in particular *The Vice*. However, the exemplar of the hybrid procedural, which naturally nestles between the 'police deviance' and 'deviant police' tale in Reiner's taxonomy, is *Between the Lines*, which ran on BBC TV for three series between 1992 and 1994. Perhaps more than any other TV cop show, *Between the Lines* redefined the contours of a copland in which, to borrow Cashmore's words:

> Older simplifications were replaced by complexity: the good lie and deceive almost as often as the bad, deals are done instead of justice being served, culprits do not always get caught. (1994: 154)

In the latter respect, at least, *Between the Lines* invites comparison with its near-contemporary, the American TV cop show, *Homicide: Life on the Streets*, although Green (2000) is probably accurate in claiming that *Between the Lines* and other British police series of the 1990s, through the frequently less-than-heroic professional exploits and personal lives of their main protagonists, challenged the ideology of law and order in ways that American commercial TV offerings ultimately do not. Discussing Tony Clark's marital infidelities and the manner in which he compromises his own investigations, Green notes:

> What is truly political is the revelation of how thoroughgoing, how all enveloping is the life of secrecy, betrayal, and anti-social solidarity that the police are forced to lead. A man whose job it is to root out lies is himself constantly telling lies, and does not even notice the contradictions. (2000: 218)

Between the Lines tackled head on the double-edged morality which police work so often invokes, a theme captured tellingly in a remark made by Clark's boss, the villainous Chief Superintendent John Deakin in 'The Chill Factor', the final episode of the programme's first series. Turning to the Chief Constable of Wessex (described earlier by Harry Naylor as a 'high calibre turnip-top' to underline the reference to the real life Operation Countryman investigation) Deakin declares, 'The Met's never been cleaner, I can tell you that for a fact. It's also a fact that our clear-up rate for crime is at an all-time low. What conclusion you draw…is entirely up to you.'

As alluded to at the end of Chapter 5, the storylines in *Between the Lines* focused on tensions between personal and professional ethics, a kind of cognitive dissonance which affects not only those under investigation, but also those investigating them. The slippery slope of 'moral flexibility' is seen to exist at all levels of the police hierarchy, from the street cops, through the management cops and beyond bureaucracy to their political masters. 'Big boys' rules' rather than guilty pleas and due process of law ultimately define the way that the politics of policing are played out, as is reflected in an exhortation from a senior officer to Clark in episode 4 of the first series: 'Our elders and betters want a result, so get one!' In the final episode of series two, when confronted in custody with serious criminal allegations, Clark's own defiant challenge to his accusers of 'Prove it', echoes precisely the response that he had received earlier in the series when interrogating a detective suspected of murdering his wife. The collusive culture of the canteen, associated primarily with the lower ranks closing in under threat of external scrutiny, was thus seen in both series one and two to extend to CIB itself, raising as Brunsdon (2000: 200) suggests, anxious questions not only about 'whodunnit?', but also about 'who can be trusted to find out?' and, most importantly, 'who *is* accountable?' Until the 1990s, the British TV police show's consideration of the politics of the police had been at best incomplete and partial. While many had dealt with low to middle level internal police politics and, as often happened in community police dramas like the 1980's *The Bill*, with *local* political issues, they had rarely addressed the complexities of high command, accountability and the various external political influences on policing. Through intelligent 'news-responsive' storylines (Brunsdon, 2000: 211) that bore 'close resemblance to real events' (Cashmore, 1994: 155), *Between the Lines* and other hybrids have extended the scope of the British TV cop show to consider moral and managerial dilemmas in policing, handling such controversial areas as gender, race and sexual politics with a degree of realism and critical awareness that none of their predecessors had matched. Machiavellian manipulation is a recurrent theme in *Between the Lines*, as evidenced by the episodes in series two which featured an autocratic provincial chief constable who, in order to protect his own reputation and that of his alcoholic deputy (convincingly played by James Cosmo), sets out systematically to scapegoat both his woman assistant chief constable and a male chief superintendent after a public order event goes disastrously out of control with tragic consequences redolent of the Hillsborough stadium disaster. In another storyline, a young white woman police officer accuses her male sergeant of sexual harassment. However, audience expectations are reversed when it emerges that the officer concerned is both black and an extremely dedicated professional. There is a further twist when it turns out that the complaint has been orchestrated by a racist and sexist senior officer who not only wants the 'Carribean cousin' out of his division, but also has designs on the woman constable himself. As Brunsdon argues

> ...what is perhaps most significant about *Between the Lines* is the clarity with which it addressed key issues of policing in the 1980s and 1990s – civil disorder, drugs, corruption, freemasonry, secondary picketing, use of informants, racism and sexual discrimination within the service – and the ambivalence which it maintained about the strategies used to address these issues. (2000: 212)

Though not without justification regarded by some as a 'series too far', the third and least successful outing of *Between the Lines* in 1994 explored various forms of plural policing, including the role of the security services 'five' (MI5) and 'six' (MI6), by focusing on turf wars, mutual mistrust and the strangely symbiotic relationships involving them, the police, private investigators, arms trade entrepreneurs and political extremists. The main protagonists, Clark, Naylor, Connell and Deakin, were no longer part of the public police, but have made the ultimate post modern police career move are now operating instead on the fringes of a shadowy world of 'fuzzy' policing, where the ends almost always justify the means. Though it became increasingly challenging to suspend one's disbelief, the final series of *Between the Lines* did, however, develop some brave, hard-hitting and, as it turns out, some remarkably prescient stories about the rise of pan-European fascism and transnational terrorist networks which, a decade later, have considerable contemporary resonance. Indeed, *Between the Lines* can be seen as having paved the way for the arrival of new hybrid procedural dramas which focus on policing by agencies other than the public police, such as *The Knock* (set inside a Customs specialist investigation unit) and, more recently, *Spooks*, which follows the work of an MI5 counter-terrorism section. As in the opening title sequence of *Between the Lines*, the frequent use of split-screen images in subsequent hybrid procedurals (including US variants like *24*) can be interpreted as a kind of visual metaphor for the fragmented and rather paranoid nature of policing in the risk society which, as Sparks suggests, is 'pitting heroic individuals against an establishment that is not merely cumbersome but a compromised and no longer trustworthy arm of an increasingly secret state' (1995: 64).

Representations of police culture and diversity

For many years, the dominant lead characters in British TV cop shows (as in real-life police organisations) have tended to be white, Anglo-Saxon men. The casting of Jill Gascoine in *The Gentle Touch* and Stephanie Turner – later replaced by Anna Carteret – in *Juliet Bravo* in traditionally male, senior positions, did briefly bring women police out of their traditional 'supportive' supporting roles and into the foreground, something which occurred rather more frequently in the United States through ground-breaking programmes like *Policewoman* and *Cagney and Lacey*. However, a significant advance came in the 1990s with Helen Mirren's inspired performance as DCI Jane Tennison in Granada TV's *Prime Suspect*, a programme which former Deputy Chief Constable John Stalker claimed 'comes closest to the atmosphere of the CID offices I grew up in: tough, taciturn and sexist' (*Sunday Times*, 20 September 1992). Stalker's remark is, of course, corroborated by the findings of over thirty years of Anglo-American social scientific studies of policework, which have served to define and refine the constituent characteristics of cop culture, a world-view framed by a recurring set of common themes, in particular moral conservatism, a sense of mission, social isolation and action-centred machismo (Chan, 1997; Reiner, 2000b). The culture of the police canteen and the after-work alcohol consumption and associated humour suggest a social environment pervaded by a cult of 'hegemonic masculinity' (Eaton, 1995; Walklate, 2000), which makes policework, in Jennifer Brown's assessment, 'sexually atypical employment' for women (Brown, 2000: 254), and consequently problematic on many levels. As Brown suggests:

> The strong masculine ethos of policing places great emphasis on mutual support and solidarity amongst rank and file officers. This may work powerfully in favour of those who belong to the majority social categories of white male. However, for those who are different, or 'other' such as from the ethnic minorities or women, the informal culture places additional burdens on officers and excludes them from the informal support systems. (2000: 259–60)

The existence and persistence of widespread discrimination and sexual harassment within and by the police service has been attested to by countless academic studies, journalistic exposés and official reports, among them the Macpherson Report (1999), which indicted the police service with being 'institutionally racist'. Several high-profile race and sex discrimination cases brought by serving officers did much to elevate issues of equal opportunities on the policing agenda (Walklate, 2000). Perhaps more than any other event, the case brought by former Assistant Chief Constable Alison Halford (at the time Britain's highest ranking woman officer) drew attention to the 'glass ceilings' and 'greasy poles' facing women throughout their police service careers. Although by 2002, Britain had acquired in Maria Wallis of Devon and Cornwall its fourth woman chief constable (Ford, 2002), that still meant that over 98 per cent of chief constable equivalent positions were held by men, and only one of them (an assistant commissioner in the Metropolitan Police) was from an ethnic minority background (Povey and Rundle, 2001). It remains a fact that, elsewhere within the police service, women are still significantly under-represented in many specialist departments and in the ranks above sergeant. Home Office figures reveal that while women accounted for just over one-quarter of all police officer recruitment in England and Wales during 2001, only 3 per cent of all women in the service held the rank of inspector or above, the corresponding figure for men being 8 per cent (Povey and Rundle, 2001). The dominant masculine ethos of policing is continually implicated as a major contributory factor. It is rooted in an occupational culture of which the then Chief Constable of Surrey Ian Blair commented, 'even at its best [it] is not fitted to handle the disparate and shifting requirements of modern society' (Travis, 1999).

A job for 'unsuitable' women?

Against this real-life backdrop of less than equal opportunities within policing, in televisual terms, women's – or, at any rate, *white* women's – police careers might appear to have 'taken off' over the last decade or so, with the depiction of strong women characters occupying positions of power and influence within the police organisation, such as Assistant Chief Constable (ACC) Anne Stewart and Detective Suprintendent Rose Penfield in Anglia TV's *The Chief*, for example. In 1991, Lynda La Plante's *Prime Suspect* dramas propelled DCI Jane Tennison into the thick of police culture in the traditionally male role of senior investigating officer in charge of a serial murder inquiry, having not only to achieve in terms of solving the case, but also in confronting and overcoming the resentment and hostility of her almost exclusively male team. The impact of the character and the 'reality rating' of the series were heightened by being based on the experiences of real-life DCI Jackie Malton, who assisted La Plante in her research (Eaton, 1995). In the original *Prime Suspect*, Tennison's gender and assertions about her sexuality are initially used as a means with which to challenge her professional competence, especially by the disgruntled Sergeant Otley (Tom Bell) who resorts to the time-(dis)honoured cop culture tactic of suggesting to his murder squad colleagues that Tennison might be lesbian. Tennison is dedicated to her job and, in professional terms, she succeeds in progressing from being seen as a 'bitch' or 'dyke' to becoming a well respected 'guv'nor', earning the loyalty and support of her male colleagues. She does so by bringing to her role a combination of the traditionally 'masculine' traits of deter-mination and detective prowess, complemented by the stereotypically 'feminine' skills of empathy and intuition (Brunsdon, 2000). However, though Tennison's professional progression is ultimately successful, her private life is anything but. As Eaton notes:

> Closer inspection shows that the triumphs achieved by Jane Tennison are bought at a high price: a successful detective but not a successful woman. Of course it may be argued that this is merely an accurate depiction. Professional women are frequently expected to act as men without the supportive domestic infrastructure, and to act as women within their private lives, providing that structure for

others regardless of professional commitments. Women do not easily fit into structures designed to celebrate masculinity in the form endorsed by the police subculture. (1995: 175)

Prime Suspects II and *III* immersed Tennison in cases which explored two further dimensions of equal opportunities discourse within policework: *Prime Suspect II* tackled racism inside the police service, while *Prime Suspect III* raised issues concerning male child sexual abuse.

There are many parallels to be drawn between Jane Tennison and Jane Penhaligon in Jimmy McGovern's *Cracker* and Pat North in La Plante's more recent offering *Trial and Retribution,* each representing a woman whose evident competence within the male world of policework is set against a backdrop of 'failure' in personal terms – typically failure to conform to the gender stereotypes of domestic partner or mother. In *The Chief,* ACC Anne Stewart's marriage eventually breaks down as the demands of being loyal to the Eastland Police overtake her support for her housefather husband and their two children. A similar situation arises in *Between the Lines* for Maureen Connell, whose character broke new ground in terms of examining the sexual politics of policing, by being 'outed' as lesbian. Mo's relationship comes under immense strain as she increasingly prioritises her work relationships and loyalties to Clark and Naylor over her devotion to her partner and their home life. As we noted in Chapter 5, what is interesting in these series is the portrayal of women exhibiting similar character flaws as male police characters, such as Tony Clark in *Between the Lines*, Pat Chappel in *The Vice* and Mike Walker in *Trial and Retribution*, characters whose ultimately self-destructive dedication to the job come to epitomise the pain of police culture. Therein lies the paradox.

The status and profile of women characters in TV police drama has certainly increased in the years following *Prime Suspect*, BBC's *Merseybeat* with a woman superintendent in charge of a police division being one of the more recent examples. By reversing traditional expectations in placing women characters into such high-profile police roles, programme-makers are afforded the opportunity to challenge gendered stereotypes, question sexual politics and to cast a critical eye over the intransigence of the male-dominated police culture. All of these things have happened – however, a cost-benefit analysis of the effects of acceptance and competence in the televisual policing environment continues – as in real life – to reveal significantly gendered differences. Strong, successful, senior women police characters are almost always 'masculinised': policework in the end is not so much an unsuitable job for a woman, but a job for 'unsuitable' women. Assertive senior women officers are often shown (as are senior male police characters) to be supported at work by more 'conventional' women, as is Jane Tennison by the gofer character of Maureen in *Prime Suspect* (Brunsdon, 2000: 207). The situation is compounded by there being very few if any examples of male characters in police dramas exhibiting 'feminine' characteristics. The partners of senior policewomen as in *The Chief* and *Merseybeat*, however, are shown quite clearly to be long-suffering and self-sacrificing men dealing with disproportionate domestic demands and who have to cope with the effects of familial commitments being constantly disrupted by their partner's work. At the same time, while there are still few male police characters in TV copland who are depicted as voluntarily putting marital and family responsibilities ahead of the job or after-work socialising, there have been some notable examples since the 1990s. Sergeant Lewis's constant commitment to 'Mrs Lewis and the kids' is quite the antithesis of the eponymous *Inspector Morse*'s rather selfish and sad singleton existence, while in *Between the Lines* Harry Naylor's devotion to his terminally ill wife and their shared love of ballroom dancing struck an unbearably poignant chord. The fact that one can now even begin to identify such male characters in police drama should be welcomed as a positive and long overdue development. However, while recent TV cop drama may have done much to raise awareness of issues of sexism and discrimination within the police service, in the final analysis, by its tendency to 'masculinise' women police characters, it arguably restores and reinforces the legitimacy of the dominant male ethos of police culture. Thus, 'equal' opportunities appear to exist mainly in the sense that the loneliness of the microwaveable meal for one, the emptiness of the emotionless casual sexual encounter, the discomfort of living with a noisy conscience and the inability of alcohol to dull the pain are now more regularly depicted as almost inevitable costs to be experienced by both female and male police characters.

Demographic deficits

With regard to representations of race and ethnicity, once again we would have to look to American film and TV to locate prominent examples of positive profiling, for David Yip as the *Chinese Detective* (1981–82), remains to this day one of only a handful of ethnic minority police leads on British TV. While in Chapter 5 we mentioned some recent examples of teams of detectives which include ethnic minority officers as a means of connoting cultural diversity and inclusiveness, the televisual portrayal of police officers has generated far fewer positive role models for black and Asian people than for white women, though with the departure of DI Burnside from *The Bill* in 1994, we did see the arrival of its first (and only) black woman detective inspector, Sally Johnson, as his replacement. Typically, however, ethnic minority women characters, like the majority of their real-life counterparts, are compartmentalised as career constables. In British TV police drama, it has been unusual for ethnic minority officers to be promoted beyond the rank of sergeant, though interestingly, in reality, a slightly higher percentage of all male ethnic minority officers currently serving in England and Wales have achieved the rank of inspector or above (almost 5 per cent) than the corresponding proportion (3 per cent) of all policewomen (Povey and Rundle, 2001). Over the years, *The Bill* has regularly featured a small complement of black and Asian officers of both genders, though such characters are generally confined to the ranks of uniformed or detective constable. However, as Jim Pines suggests, ethnic minority characters in *The Bill* have usually been deployed in somewhat predictable plotlines that juxtapose black officer and black-related crime and/or black officer with racially motivated community tensions, and this can serve on occasions to emphasise 'racial caricature rather than "realism" ' (1995: 70). However, in March 2002, following a spate of arson attacks in Sun Hill, Asian DS Vik Singh was portrayed as himself inflaming racial unrest, ignoring the cautionary advice of his black DC, Danny Glaze, with ultimately tragic consequences for the local community and several of their Sun Hill colleagues (http://www.thebill.com/episode). As his character biography states:

> When racial taunts become too much for Singh he hospitalizes a white supremacist suspect. Confronted with the truth [DCI] Meadows suspends him pending CIB's investigation. Rather than face up to the consequences of his actions, he resigns with immediate effect. (http://www.thebill.com/characters)

Despite adhering to what Pines refers to as the exigencies of the 'race relations' narrative (1995: 76), Vik Singh can be seen as having bucked convention by presenting a rare example of a flawed black cop 'hero'. Pines is accurate in his analysis that black officers in British TV fiction have tended to be portrayed as 'noble' individuals, 'whose mission is to clean up criminalized black neighbourhoods' (1995: 74), or who like DS Oswalde in *Prime Suspect II* struggle stoically to rise above the racism and prejudice of their white colleagues. In many regards ethnic minority characters – and especially ethnic minority men – appear qualitatively under-represented in TV drama as law enforcers when comparisons are made with the real-life demographics of the police service. Yet, at the same time, there must remain more than a reasonable suspicion that black and other ethnic minorities remain quantitatively over-represented in the character roles of lawbreakers when compared to real-life patterns of offending. As we suggested in Chapter 2, there is some important research to be done in this area.

Not enough chiefs

Before the 1990s, the British TV police procedural maintained an almost exclusive focus on the 'federated ranks', i.e. from constable up to chief inspector. Senior police officers tended to be kept very much in the background, the 'old man' upstairs, detached from the 'real police work' going on 'out there'. Even in the 1980s *The Bill*, in which Chief Superintendent Brownlow, the former Sun Hill divisional commander, appeared not infrequently, he featured mainly as a mediator between the competing aims and claims of his CID, community liaison and uniformed operations inspectors and chief inspectors. That, and attending the occasional heated community meeting on the Jasmine Allen estate, was about as political as the politics of the police got. Barring the occasional forays from Area HQ to Sun Hill of a commander or assistant commissioner, there were simply not enough chiefs shown in TV drama to reflect the prominence in real-life of the powerful and high-profile chief officers that we drew attention to in Chapter 3. However, in the 1990s, dramas like *Prime Suspect* and *Between the Lines* extended the scope of the cop show with their portrayals of conniving commanders and the kind of murky struggles for power and influence that occupy the higher echelons of the service. Anglia TV's *The Chief* (1990–95) was mould-breaking in having as its main protagonist the Chief Constable of the Eastland Police, a fictional force located in East Anglia. In the first three series, Chief Constable John Stafford (Tim Piggot-Smith) came across as a hard-nosed yet liberal-minded career bureaucrat, an image which was, at least in part, cultivated through a period that the actor spent shadowing the late Sir John Hoddinott, former Chief Constable of Hampshire. When the Stafford character left Eastland to head Europol, his successor was dynamic DAC Alan Cade whom the actor Martin Shaw modelled on Peter Ryan, the then real-life Chief Constable of Norfolk (Haining, 1995).

Throughout *The Chief*'s run, which at its peak attracted audiences of almost 12 million, John Alderson, former Chief Constable of Devon and Cornwall, acted as the series' police adviser. Authenticity was again further heightened by the news-responsiveness of its storylines, which, as in *Between the Lines*, closely tracked some of the pressing policing concerns of the moment: prison riots, animal rights protestors, neo-nazi groups, illegal immigration, drugs trafficking, environmental crime and the unregulated private security sector. Both Stafford and Cade were seen to operate in a highly charged political environment, often clashing with manipulative Home Office mandarins, the security services and career politicians, while at the same time having to guard against unfriendly fire from other agents of the establishment, including obstructive Inspectors of Constabulary and disloyal deputies. Each chief conveyed in different ways the loneliness of occupying the desk where the buck stops. As mentioned above, *The Chief* was also unusual for the time in having among its principal players two senior women officers shown to be within striking distance of the top job. The ACC Anne Stewart character faced in fiction the same glass-ceiling that the Alison Halford case had highlighted in reality when she failed to achieve promotion to deputy chief constable. *The Chief* brought to the small screen for the first time credible portrayals of very senior officers coping with the pressures of high-profile, politically sensitive public roles, while at the same time having to contend with problems and difficulties in their own private lives and family relationships. In contrast to the reaction to *Z Cars* some forty years earlier, there were no reports of overnight dashes to Anglia TV by apoplectic ACPO members to protest about gross misrepresentation.

In assessing contemporary TV copland's handling of police culture and diversity, we can see that things have moved on in many significant respects from earlier stereotypes and the 'blue-collar' feel of the traditional police procedural. As we noted in Chapter 4, representing diversity in the earliest TV cop shows was more or less limited to the 'four of a kind' formula, which brought together and to the fore English, Scots, Irish and Welsh white male police officers, while women characters remained very much in the home or, if at work, were kept in clearly subordinate, supporting and supportive roles. Even by the early 1980s, *The Bill* could still be said to be little more than '*Dixon* with different dialects', albeit with accents more representative of the modern metropolitan mix. However, as we have attempted to demonstrate, things have changed since the 1990s, with the emergence of dramas that injected complexity into the police procedural by reversing role expectations and casting characters contrary to stereotype. The boundaries of diversity in police drama have more recently been extended to include neglected aspects of sexual orientation, as well as gender and ethnicity, with the appearance of openly gay male police characters, such as DC Fraser in *Taggart* and Sergeant Craig Gilmore in *The Bill*. However, the invisibility of disability in TV representations of policing is significant. The portrayal of an officer recovering from a stroke in *Homicide: Life on the Streets*, and the effects of a progressive eye disease on Detective Chief Inspector Ross Tanner (Clive Owen) in *Second Sight*, are rare instances of engagement

with such issues. In summary, though the discourse of equal opportunities is now an established ingredient in TV copland as is the case
in real-life policing, there is very considerable progress still to be made in
both domains in terms of positive profiling and the celebration of cultural
diversity.

Reiner revisited: continuing the dialectic

In concluding this chapter and this section of the book, we will attempt to
extend Reiner's (1994) dialectical discussion of cop drama (see Table 6.2).
Although in Chapter 4, we argued that Reiner possibly understated the
significance of *Z Cars*, we accept that his conceptualisation of it as a
'transitional text' is by no means invalid, as *Z Cars* – at least in the earliest
series – brought in rougher edges to the community cop drama of which
Dixon was the apotheosis. *Z Cars* in many senses prepared the ground for
The Sweeney, an uncompromising, 'let 'em have it' drama set in an anomic
London undergoing a perceived real-life law and order crisis (Chapter 5).
The Sweeney was the antithesis of *Dixon* and heralded the heyday of an
overtly macho, controlling image of policing that captured the mood of
1970s Britain and which was echoed in other programmes like *The
Professionals*. Mirroring developments in the United States, a more
feminised portrayal of British policing arrived in the forms of *Juliet Bravo*
and *The Gentle Touch*, which together tipped the emphasis back towards a
more caring community-centred form of policing, paving the way for
the 'synthesis' that was 1980s (old) *The Bill* which, suggests Reiner (1994),
established a state of equilibrium, achieving a balance between care and
control, and between bobby and detective.

Table 6.2   Reiner revisited

Defining Drama	Status	Representation
Dixon of Dock Green	Thesis	Care
Z Cars	Transitional text	Rougher edges
The Sweeney	Antithesis	Control
Juliet Bravo	Transitional text	Gentler touches
The (Old) *Bill*	Synthesis = New thesis	Care–control
Prime Suspect	Transitional text	Cop culture
Between the Lines	Antithesis	Corruption
Cracker	Transitional text	Appliance of science
The (New) *Bill*	New synthesis	Care–control–corruption

Following in the Hegelian dialectical tradition, *The Bill* as synthesis in turn becomes the new thesis for the 1980s. However, since then the drama has been reinvented to come into alignment with wider changes that were occurring in 1990s TV copland and, of course, associated shifts in audience expectations. The defining transitional text in terms of upsetting the fulchrum of the late 1980s care–control equilibrium was Lynda La Plante's *Prime Suspect* which injected a massive dose of cop culture into the TV police genre, right at a time when issues of sexism and racism were coming to the fore in real-life policing. As we have suggested, *Prime Suspect* and its contemporary series *The Chief* also began to address some glaring demographic deficits in police drama, including extending the genre's scope to include policing at all levels of the organisation. TV police drama became more overtly political and critical and it was time for the arrival of the antithesis of much of what had gone on previously. It came in the form of John Wilsher's award-winning *Between the Lines* which we would argue, was *the* defining drama that changed the contours of British TV copland, by embedding the central constituent of the hybrid procedural, namely the 'apple crumble' effect. No longer would televisual representations of policing continue to proceed along a simple two-dimensional care–control axis. *Between the Lines* added a third dimension – pervasive corruption.

We must next acknowledge, as does Brunsdon (2000), the emergence in the mid–late 1990s of a cluster of what we might term 'medico-detective' dramas (*Dangerfield*, *Silent Witness* and *McCallum*), programmes which had as their main protagonists police surgeons and pathologists working closely with the police. These forensic medical characters were liberated from their traditional roles of providing gobbets of gallows humour at crime scenes and autopsies, as in *Taggart* and *Morse*, to enhance the ethics of an investigative process in which, as *Between the Lines* and other hybrid procedurals had revealed, much evidence is routinely 'doctored' by the police. As Brunsdon suggests, there is a sense in which this dynamic echoes her own question about 'who can be *trusted* to police?' In a TV copland unable to deliver an unambiguous response to that question, there is perhaps inevitably a discernible 'move towards the medicalisation of crime within the crime series' (Brunsdon, 2000: 216). Interestingly, developments in American cop shows exhibit similar trends. After the more complex and ambiguous representations of 'policing as social science' in dramas such as *NYPD* and *Homicide* (Poniewozik, 2000), the 'forensic empiricism' of dramas like *Law and Order* and *CSI: Crime Scene Investigation* seem to have returned some of the certainties of science to TV policework. In the context of our endeavour to update Reiner's dialectic, *Cracker* would be our candidate for transitional text. As we discussed in the previous chapter, Fitz not only embodies all of the flaws of cop culture, but also extends the iconography of the police procedural to embrace the field of forensic psychology, in particular offender profiling which, being based on probabilities, is arguably the quintessential scientific aid to policing in the risk society.

Our nomination for new synthesis would (unremarkably) be the 'new' *The Bill* that has emerged in the late 1990s, early 2000. *The Bill* began to feature some dangerous and disturbingly corrupt police characters in PC Eddie Santini and DS Don Beech, who between them systematically engaged in every conceivable form of rule-breaking and corruption, including drug-dealing and murder. At the same time, more 'ordinary' police characters began to acquire and develop serious moral failings and character flaws: PC Jim Carver, for example, was revealed to be an out of control 'alcoholic' while PC 'Smiffy' Smith was shown to harbour extreme right-wing political sympathies. Don Beech's escapades finally brought about the downfall of Mr Brownlow and the subsequent cleaning up of Sun Hill nick. While Beech escaped justice 'down under', a new broom arrived in the form of Superintendent Chandler, initially depicted as a high-flying, tough and incorruptible senior officer, fixated on performance management and quality of service. However, Chandler turns out to have a 'Clintonesque weakness around women' (http:// thebill.com/characters/ch_chandler.html) and by spring 2002, the 'apple crumble' effect in *The* 'new' *Bill* is pervasive: DCI Meadows and DC Mickey Webb are conspiring to destroy Chandler's career, just as the superintendent embarks on an increasingly indiscreet affair with the manipulative DS Debbie McAllister. Meanwhile, WPC Cass Rickman is doing drugs, Sergeant Matt Boyden is homophobic and PC Des Taviner, the person responsible for throwing the fatal petrol bomb that devastates Sun Hill and its officers, is desperately trying to cover his tracks and deflect the blame. A press release dated 15 March 2002 reveals that the programme's 'secret weapon' is its story consultant Jackie Malton, the former DCI who worked with Lynda La Plante on *Prime Suspect* (http:// www.thebill.com/news).

Ever the synthesis, *The Bill* has come to define the virtually real territory of a contemporary TV copland, where the moral certainties of *Dixon* are long gone and television cop heroes have become people whose virtue is relative rather than absolute. As Reiner put it, 'Their moral status is contestable, and has to be established anew in each narrative' (2000b: 162). As Robards suggested, society may well still look to the TV cop to arbitrate between right and wrong, but these days audiences know only too well that, as in their own real lives, the distinction between the two is often blurred, that right does not always triumph, and that sometimes, maybe even most of the time, the bad guys, who may be otherwise 'good' cops – will get away with it. In answer to the question 'How can I trust you?', ex-DI Claire Stanton, in *The Bill* spin-off *Beech is Back*, states 'I was a police officer, I know how to get away with things'. Audiences will continue to 'commute' between the various forms of fictional police representation, from nostalgia trips like *Heartbeat* to the darker world of hybrids like *The Vice*. However, these days viewers in search of moral certainty are perhaps more likely to find it not in the fictional police procedural, but instead in 'faction' in the format of the police 'reality' show, which we will discuss in the next chapter.

Part Three
Factions

Chapter 7

That's infotainment

Introduction

Inevitably, the growth of technology and in particular advances in digital media have altered the face of visual entertainment. The ever-diminishing size of cameras and microphones have facilitated new forms of television that, along with film, are soon to become widely available on broadband Internet services.[1] These developments have also led to changes in factual programming, in which there has been an increased hybridisation of the documentary. The terms documentary drama, the drama-documentary, infotainment and faction have all been used to describe predominantly factual programmes with dramatic, reconstructive elements. One recent development of this hybrid format has been 'reality television', which Kilborn and Izod describe as:

> … the mode in which television packaging makes the most sophisticated intervention in actuality-based production as it seeks to highlight the sense of shared experience or lived reality. (1997: 85)

Germaine Greer has commented that 'Reality television is not the end of civilisation as we know it: it *is* civilisation as we know it. It is popular culture at its most popular' (Greer, 2001: 1). These programmes have continued to increase both in popularity and their regularity on British television. The 2001 series of *Big Brother* topped Channel Four's audience ratings for its eleven-week run, averaging around five million viewers (British Audience Research Board). In August 2001, there were seven reality television shows broadcast on terrestrial television and a further 13 on cable and satellite channels (British Audience Research Board), not including a cable station dedicated entirely to the genre called, imaginatively, *Reality TV.* There has also been an edition of the quiz show *The Weakest Link* made up of contestants from reality television shows.

This blurring of the boundaries between documentary, soap opera and fiction has predominantly taken three broad forms. First is the docu-soap, in which the audience watch the weekly exploits of a particular group of people: for example shop assistants (*Lakesiders*), people on holiday (*Ibiza Uncovered, Carribean Uncovered*), learner drivers (*Driving School*) or residents of a particular area (*Paddington Green*). Second is an emerging group of programmes loosely termed 'biovision': game shows in which volunteers are put in artificial living environments and required to carry out tasks. Although the BBC was the first to schedule a prime time slot for such a programme in January 2000 (*Castaway* about a group of people living on a bleak island), the populist forerunner of this form of reality television in Britain was *Big Brother.* In this programme, 12 people lived in a house and were filmed 24 hours a day, the television audience evicting one housemate each week. Since the phenomenal success of the first series in 2000, a flood of imitations has appeared: *Survivor, The Mole, Temptation Island* and *Jail Break* among them. Third, and some of the earliest examples of the genre, are reality television programmes that follow the emergency and rescue services, including *999, Police, Camera, Action!, Children's Hospital, Jimmy's* and several imported shows from the United States including *Cops* and *America's Most Wanted.*

It is this third category of reality television that concerns us here, in particular those programmes that either use surveillance footage from closed circuit television or police cameras and the fly-on-the-wall documentary about police work, sometimes referred to as the 'media ride-along'. Such programmes raise several questions that include: what is the relationship between the police and television in the making of these reality TV police shows? What effect do such programmes have on the police, the suspect and the victim? What are the consequences for justice in the eyes of the audience? What is the appeal of such programmes?

Cops on the box

We have already seen in earlier chapters how advances in production and filming techniques have been responsible for the changing face of police drama. In the 1960s, *Z Cars* injected pace and authenticity into the police drama with its six cameras, screen backdrops and outside recording. The fly-on-the-wall techniques used in the documentary *Police* and *The Bill* since the early 1980s and taken to their extreme in *Cops* in the late 1990s have altered visual representations of law enforcement. Similarly, it was the development of lightweight cameras and synchronised sound recording that significantly aided the development of reality television. Fetveit (1999) notes that the reality television show relies on three types of visual evidence, 'authentic footage from camera crews observing arrests or rescue operations, footage from surveillance videos and recordings (often by amateurs) of dramatic accidents and dangerous situations' (Fetveit, 1999: 792). The reality police show is predominantly shot using camera crews and surveillance videos. These series originated in the United States in the late 1980s, where programmes such as *Rescue 911*, *Real Life Heroes* and *On Screen: Emergency Rescue* were developed by the major networks, CBS and Fox (Kilborn, 1994: 426). One of the earliest examples on British television was *Police, Camera, Action!* (1995) in which police surveillance footage taken from patrol cars and helicopters is broadcast anchored by ex-ITN news reader Alistair Stewart. The series justifies its existence by stressing its safety message:

> [*Police, Camera, Action!*] captures on camera moments of motoring madness and has earned plaudits from police and drivers alike for its powerful safety message...There's a chance to see the latest police technology in action and reckless drivers caught on camera. (http://www.carltontv.co.uk/data/policecameraaction/)

Since the success of the programme (the series has been nominated for a BAFTA and has run for seven years) other programmes have evolved also concerned with the work of the police. These include Carlton Television's *Blues and Twos* that used miniature cameras placed on the uniforms of rescue crews, and in November 1995 a two-hour live programme following four police forces around the country called *Police Action Live* (Hill, 2000).

Despite their justifications of public interest, the reality police show has encountered considerable criticism. The Independent Television Commission considered real crime programmes to be 'very patchy indeed' and 'a bit tacky' (*The Independent*, April 1996). Similarly, the Broadcast Standards Council in its Annual Report 1996 reported an increase in the number of complaints about both *Police, Camera, Action!* and *Blues and Twos*. In June 1996, the Council upheld a complaint against *Blues and Twos* for screening footage of an 82-year-old woman and her 85 year-old husband after a road crash (*The Times*, 10 July 1996). As well as these ethical concerns, there are questions about reality programming contributing to the decline in broadcasting standards and the increase in tabloid television:

> Whether earnestly serving the public interest or cheekily amusing the public, it [television] is engaged in a drip-drip erosion of codes of fair dealing and consent which were framed before the camcorder revolution and the arrival of the micro camera. (Dugdale, in Kilborn, 1994: 436)

Police, camera, faction

While infotainment programmes such as *Police, Camera, Action!* and *The World's Dumbest Criminals* rely on surveillance footage, perhaps the most important development has been the media ride-along. These programmes, mostly imported from the United States, are based around cameras that follow the police in and out of their patrol car. The footage is bumpy and chaotic where 'the white noise from police radios and accidental environmental sounds testifies to the authenticity of recordings' (Fetveit, 1999: 792). Chase, arrest and accompanying interviews with the victim are all essential elements for the cop show ride-along. These are accompanied by slow motion, oft-repeated sequences and dramatic voice-over. Fetveit comments that it is 'the audio-visual evidence as much as the story' (Fetveit, 1999: 794) which is a distinguishing feature of this form of reality television.

Such shows represent a shift in the traditional form of documentary, blurring the lines between fact and fiction. Holland (1996) suggests that the notion of the documentary to inform and be primarily concerned with quality rather than audience size has been replaced by the documentary as 'television's prime dramatic medium, targeting moments of conflict and crisis' (Holland, 1996: 23). Corner (2000) too argues that these programmes represent a new further function of the documentary: documentary as diversion:

> Propagandist, expositional or analytic goals are exchanged for modes of intensive or relaxed diversion – the primary viewing activity is on looking and overhearing, perhaps aligned to events by intermittent commentary. (Corner, 2000)

Like Holland, he suggests that traditional forms of documentary journalism – inquiry and radical interrogation – have been readdressed by a post-documentary format that borrows from the advertisement, drama and pop video to be 'strategically designed for the television marketplace' (Corner, 2000: 4). As noted previously, a concern exists among writers that this form of reality television programming is part of the downgrading of public service broadcasting, emphasising the dramatic and the entertaining over the wider social and political questions:

> Though evoking a strong sense of events occurring in the 'here and now', these reality bites effectively bracket out those wider areas of social concern to which classic documentary attached so much importance. (Kilborn and Izod, 1997: 157)

The thin blue line

Central to the genre of reality police shows is the relationship between the police and the media. The use of hand-held cameras and the absence of a voice-over in the media ride-along gives an impression of the 'real'. However 'masquerading as reality, these selected sequences drawn from the immediacy of live events form nothing more than stories' (Andersen, 1994: 8). The reality television cop show is another constructed representation of the police, just like *The Bill* or *Merseybeat*, where the narrative structure of events is determined by the producer not the police officer. Chase and arrest are edited to produce an exhilarating experience for the viewer. The journey begins and ends in the patrol car with the officers, a neat circular frame on which the action can be hung.

> Say what you like, *Police, Camera, Action!* is 100 percent true real life…where every police driver shows perfect judgement and every car thief is a crap navigator who immediately turns down a cul-de-sac. (Hamilton, 1998)

Reality television cannot then be treated as such, 'The situations are contrived and the protagonists are handpicked' (Greer, 2001: 2). In a content analysis of reality-based police shows, Oliver (1994) found that violent crime was 'over-represented' with 87 per cent of criminal suspects being associated with violent crime compared with 1991 FBI statistics of 13 per cent of crimes indexed as violent. Clear-up rates were also significantly higher, with 61.5 per cent cleared in the television shows compared with 18 per cent in FBI statistics. Notwithstanding the well-documented difficulties with content analyses as a research methodology

(Sparks, 1987; Barker, 1988; Winston, 1990) Oliver's findings underline the modifications and alterations made in reality shows.

It is perhaps the simplification and decontextualising of events that is potentially the most troublesome. As we saw in Chapter 3, Chibnall (1977) discusses the simplification of crime news into a morality tale of good versus evil. Barak (1994) notes that '[T]he broader systematic relations of social problems are also ignored, although the symptoms are bemoaned' (Barak, 1994: 143) in reality-based police shows. No more is this true than in relation to drug-related crime as Andersen (1994) illustrates in examining an episode of the US show *Night Beat*. A white officer wrestles a black suspect to the ground following a daring chase and flying leap to apprehend the suspect: 'The cop presents his young trophy to the camera with his arm around the suspect's neck' (Andersen, 1994: 10). Following comments by the reporter about high school football and the physical prowess of the arresting officer, remarks are made about the streets being a little safer. The suspect was found in possession of cocaine with a street value of just $20. The contents and effects of such messages have been discussed in Chapter 2; however, it is interesting to note that the United States National Drug Control Strategy has concentrated more than 70 per cent of resources on law enforcement at street level. Meanwhile commentators on America's drug problem have pointed out that it is social and economic conditions that need to be most urgently addressed.

This example illustrates the problems of reality television police series. What purports to be reality is a mediated representation of such. The arguments pertaining to electronic broadcast coverage of court proceedings (see Chapter 8) may equally apply here: 'Their tools will be imagination and analysis, distortion and dramatization, comment and comparison' Mauro (1994: 12). Further evidence of the tinkering with actual events has been well documented by the printed press. In 1998, the makers of docu-soap *Driving School* admitted reconstructing an incident that one character had told them about (*The Independent*, 16 November 1998). A more pertinent example concerned a police show where a reporter in the United States discovered that the police officers on media ride-along show *American Detective* were asked by producers to repeat particular lines and were encouraged to play to the camera (Andersen, 1994: 10).

If one is to accept that television will alter police events to suit their own ratings-driven agenda, the aim, nature and role of police cooperation in making such programmes must be examined. We have seen in fiction how police officers have been represented as heroic crimefighters from the days of *Dixon of Dock Green* to *Cops*, and this has continued with reality television police shows. However, the images of the police constructed by these programmes are that of a homogeneous team, 'an abstract form of heroic consistency' (Fishman, 1999: 273) in which the crimefighter is interchangeable, a member of the team not an individual. Although such favourable representations of the police may come as no surprise, on closer examination it may be closer to cock-up than conspiracy. Reiner (2000a) identifies four reasons for the favourable portrayal of the police in the media. First, the ingredients for what makes a good story as identified by writers and producers inherently include good triumphing over evil. Second are 'formal and informal censorship pressures deriving from a variety of moral entrepreneurs' (Reiner, 2000b: 58) such as the Hays Code operating in Hollywood in the 1950s which stipulated that films should never show crime to pay. Third is the need for the media to maintain police cooperation both as advisers in fiction but more significantly as sources of crime stories, the structured access of the press discussed by Chibnall (1977).

However, the police have taken on a high media profile in recent years following several damaging reports alleging, among other things, institutional racism (Macpherson, 1999). Since the early 1990s there have been increasing steps taken by the police in controlling their media image, including the use of media professionals (Mawby, 2001). This seems to extend to the role of the police in reality TV, in which the image created may also be managed. Mawby (2001) notes how the language of police media relations centres around 'openness'. It is such an approach that constructs a trope that equates policing with crimefighting, so prevalent an image in reality police shows. Andersen (1994) talks more of the media's collusion, suggesting reality police shows 'are actually little more than products of the media's over-reliance on the entertainment value of the law enforcement establishment' (Andersen, 1994: 9), failing to take a critical stance of the work of the police on the streets.

Crimewatch UK

One aspect of reality television that has not been discussed thus far is *Crimewatch UK*. The interactive nature of the crime-solving show and the role of reconstructions are also forms of infotainment. This will be organised adapting Kilborn and Izod's (1997) three principal questions on the series: are the reconstructions of crimes a representative cross-section of crimes committed or do other criteria play a more significant role? Does the emphasis on crimes against the person in these reconstructions increase the fear of crime in the *Crimewatch UK* audience?

Third, and building upon a key theme in this chapter: what kind of relationship do the police have with the programme and what is the extent of their influence over its content?

Crimewatch UK was developed by the BBC from a German programme called *Aktenzeichen XY* ... which had been running since 1967 in the Federal Republic of Germany, Austria and Switzerland to audiences of around 20 million (Schlesinger and Tumber, 1993: 2). Whereas the German programme had included a significant number of political and terrorist crimes, *Crimewatch* took its lead from ITV's *Police Five* in which presenter Shaw Taylor always signed off with the friendly exhortation to be vigilant, 'keep 'em peeled'. Having secured the cooperation of the Association of Chief Police Officers, the first series of *Crimewatch UK* was broadcast in 1984. The format of the programme has remained relatively unchanged since its first broadcast, with one presenter, Nick Ross, having never missed a programme. Broadcast monthly, the 60-minute programme is based around three or four reconstructions of crimes on which the police have no leads. Each reconstruction features a voice-over of one of the two presenters and interviews with actual witnesses or victims. At the end of the reconstruction there is an interview with the senior investigating officer. Other regular items on the series include an update on crimes featured since the last series and 'photocall', described as 'television's answer to the wanted poster' (Ross and Cook, 1987: 111); there is also an 'incident desk' presented by two serving police officers. More recently, the series has included a feature called Aladdin's Cave in which unclaimed recovered stolen property is helpfully described by an antiques expert.

Although *Crimewatch* consistently attracts over six million viewers per show, it has received considerable criticism concerning its use of dramatic reconstruction and consequent contribution to the fear of crime. Dunkley described it as '...the most frighteningly violent programme on British Television, and quite needlessly so. Every edition is flawed by the vividly realistic re-enactment of some peculiarly horrible crime' (Dunkley, 1988: 22). It is certainly the reconstructions in the series that attract the most attention.

Undoubtedly *Crimewatch* selects those crimes for reconstruction that it believes will attract a large audience. Seetha Kumar, the BBC's creative director of crime and health and responsible for the making of *Crimewatch UK*, has stated that ratings are important: 'If I make a programme that people want to watch, I'm not ashamed about that' (*The Guardian*, 27 August 2001). The original presenters of the series, Sue Cook and Nick Ross, have also admitted that high-profile cases are likely to be featured in the programme: 'we believe it is in the programme's interests to be seen at the centre of the crime detection business' (Ross and Cook, 1987: 29), It is therefore not surprising that the majority of crimes in reconstructions are crimes against the person, for these receive wide publicity in Britain's printed media and hence demand attention from the makers of *Crimewatch UK*. Schlesinger and Tumber (1994) point out that 'by using human-interest-based tales of misfortune, it has more than a little in common with the staple of the popular press' (Schlesinger and Tumber, 1994: 142). In addressing Kilborn and Izod's first point, it would seem that selection criteria for reconstruction concerns the public consciousness of the crime and consequently the police's increased concern with solving it.

The central question surrounding the reconstructions of crime is whether the re-enactments of crime in the programme engender an increased fear of crime. While this is notoriously difficult to establish (Barker and Petley, 2001: ch. 2) many have suggested this to be the case. The Home Office, in reacting to British Crime Survey figures,[3] has suggested that *Crimewatch* created a climate of fear of crime (*The Guardian*, 7 November 2000). Donald Finlay QC, speaking at the Edinburgh Television Festival in August 2001, said he was '...genuinely concerned about the way television is using crime. It's almost becoming a sport' (*The Guardian*, 27 August 2001). *Crimewatch UK* has to perform a difficult balancing act between responsible public service broadcasting and attracting high viewing figures:

> By addressing the viewers as responsible public citizens, they attempt to enlist their support...however, [reconstructions] constitute short action-packed bursts of dramatic entertainment – valuable (from the broadcasters' point of view) in helping maintain the attention of an audience in today's increasingly competitive environment. (Kilborn and Izod, 1997: 155)

The justification for the use of so many reconstructions is twofold. First, the programme needs to attract viewers in order to have the opportunity of catching the perpetrator; and second the reconstructions are successful. Since the first programme in 1984 *Crimewatch* claims there have been 582 arrests made as a direct result of the programme (*The Independent*, 21 April 2000).

Schlesinger and Tumber argue that the police are central in the construction of *Crimewatch*, despite the programme's attempts to stress their distance: '...our professional relationship with the police does not become so embracing that it puts in jeopardy the independence of the BBC' (Ross and Cook, 1987: 156). However, without ACPO's cooperation and the continued support of the police, *Crimewatch* would not exist.

Schlesinger and Tumber describe the relationship as one of bargaining where a high degree of access is given to police records in return for public help to solve crimes. However, this is a not a bargain made on equal terms. *Crimewatch* is reliant on police information in order to make a reconstruction; in this sense it is the police who determine the content of the programme: 'although the production team exercise editorial judgement over how the cases that they reconstruct are to be presented ...their decisions take place within a well-defined framework' (Innes, 1999).

On an informal level the relationship between the programme and the police would seem to be closer than the BBC care to admit. Before transmission, all police officers staffing the phones during the programme are presented with a commemorative *Crimewatch UK* pen, 'highly prized souvenirs of a night's involvement on national TV' (Pengelly, 1999: 2).

Reality television: held in contempt?

Further concerns about the police relationship with the media relate to the suspects, witnesses, victims and defendants filmed in these programmes. Reality police shows impinge upon two particular areas: contempt of court and privacy.

Under the Contempt of Court Act 1981, reporting restrictions are placed upon the media if the publication creates a substantial risk of serious prejudice or impediment to particular proceedings and the proceedings are active. A case is defined as active under the Act if, among other things, a warrant has been issued for arrest, an arrest has been made or charges have been brought against a suspect. While there is no definition in the Act of what constitutes a 'substantial risk of prejudice', Lord Taylor has suggested that:

> ...a court should credit the jury with the will and ability to abide by the judge's direction to decide the case only on the evidence before them. The court should also bear in mind that the staying power and detail of publicity, even in cases of notoriety, are limited and that the nature of a trial is to focus the jury's minds on the evidence put before them rather than on matters outside the courtroom. (per Lord Taylor *Ex Parte The Daily Telegraph* (1993) 1 WLR 987)

In practice, contempt proceedings are brought against the media where guilt has been suggested either before or during the trial. Recent examples include the collapse of the criminal trial of Leeds United footballers Lee Bowyer and Jonathan Woodgate in April 2001 following *The Sunday Mirror's* interview with the victim's father who suggested the alleged assault was racially motivated. In the murder trial of Harold Shipman in 2000, a local radio DJ, Mark Kaye, and his traffic reporter, Judith Vause, escaped a prison sentence for contempt of court after Kaye said on air that Shipman was 'innocent until proved guilty as sin' while Vause chanted 'guilty, guilty' (*The Times*, 12 February 2000).

Reality-based police shows which reveal the identities of arrested suspects have the potential for creating a substantial risk of prejudice to the trial. If a programme broadcasts footage of a suspect being arrested, then an audience may infer guilt. This is particularly true if we consider the excision of most of the criminal justice process in police drama. A police drama-literate audience brought up with programmes like *The Sweeney* are used to the phrase 'your nicked' equating to prison for the suspect. Given the potential for such an inference of guilt, defendants whose arrest has been broadcast on a media ride-along may appeal on the grounds that the footage has prejudiced their trial. The live police documentary *Police Action Live!* broadcast by ITV in November 1995 raised such concerns: Chris Wilson, writing in *The Sunday Telegraph*, contended that 'This programme could mean a court not being able to assemble a jury who aren't prejudiced' (Wilson, 1995: 4). A greater concern is the denial of such contempt of court appeals: 'The media is taking more risks than ever before in transgressing the line that separates acceptable information from prejudicial material' (Berlins, 2000: 63).

Potentially, Article Six of The Human Rights Act 1998 introduced further restrictions on court reporting which states '...everyone is entitled to a fair and public hearing...by an independent and impartial tribunal' (Human Rights Act 1998, Article 6 (1)). Although there have been appeals based on Article 6, most notably Jon Venables and John Thompson in the James Bulger murder trial, and the 'M25 Three' case, neither were concerned primarily with the media's handling of their respective hearings. However, the suspect in the reality police show has now the Contempt of Court Act 1981 and The Human Rights Act 1998 to use in an appeal concerning the prejudicing of their trial.

It is not only the potential for reality television police shows to prejudice legal proceedings that conflicts with the law. The conduct of the media and the consequent invasions of privacy has also raised legal issues. In 1997, *The Independent* reported on a woman who had been filmed for the London Weekend Television series *Crime Monthly* without her permission (Wynn-Jones, 1997: 6). Following an attack on her, she called the police, who arrived with a camera crew. Mistaking the crew as officers recording her evidence, and in a state of shock from the attack minutes earlier, she allowed them access to her house. She subsequently received phone calls from friends and relatives consoling her, having seen the programme on television. Until the phone calls, she had no idea that she was being filmed for a television programme. This was one of several cases the civil liberty pressure group Liberty have fought on behalf of individuals who have been filmed and broadcast without their consent. Mulley (2001) argues that such media interest in the victims of crime is a form of secondary victimisation that 'can make individuals feel harassed, vulnerable, lacking control…and violated' (Mulley, 2001: 30).

Until The Human Rights Act 1998 there was no protection of privacy under English law, merely legislation that could be adapted such as trespass, the Protection from Harassment Act 1997 and the Interception of Communications Act 1985. Article Eight of The Human Rights Act 1998 offers protection 'for private and family life' and has been successfully used by Catherine Zeta Jones and Michael Douglas in suing *Hello!* magazine for using unsolicited pictures of their wedding in December 2000 (*Douglas* v. *Hello! Ltd.*, *The Times*, 16 January 2000, Court of Appeal). It remains unclear how widely individuals filmed in police shows without their prior knowledge could use the Act as a case has yet to be brought before an English court. In the Douglas case, however, Lord Justice Sedley said:

What a concept of privacy does…is accord recognition to the fact that the law has to protect not only those people whose trust has been abused but those who simply find themselves subjected to an unwanted intrusion in to their personal lives…it can recognise privacy itself as a legal principle drawn from the fundamental value of personal autonomy. (Cited in Welsh and Greenwood, 2001: 390)

In the United States, however, a case has been brought under the corresponding Fourth Amendment of the US Constitution that protects an individual's right to privacy in their own home. In May 1999, the United States Supreme Court ruled that a reporter and photographer from the *Washington Post* had violated Charles and Geraldine Wilson's Fourth Amendment right by accompanying the police during the execution of an arrest warrant (*Wilson et al.* v. *Layne, Deputy United States Marshall* May 24 1999). This decision also upheld the Ninth Circuit Court's judgment in the case of *Berger* v. *Hanlon et al.* (129 F.3d 505 9th Cir. 1997) which held that a CNN camera crew filming an authorised search of a ranch by the Fish and Wildlife Service violated the Fourth Amendment. This has had significant implications for media corporations such as Fox, the network which broadcast *Cops*, an Emmy award-winning reality television police show (Biafora and Costello, 1999). To avoid a similar ruling, shows such as *Cops* will have to get permission from home owners before the police search or arrest, a totally impractical task in the circumstances.

The Supreme Court decision is the first sign of the reinstatement of suspects' and victims' rights against the reality TV show. There is a feeling among commentators that these shows simply trample over individuals' rights in the name of entertainment:

> Constitutional assumptions about due process and civil liberties, such as protections against unwarranted search and seizure and the presumption of innocence, are antithetical to the crime-tabloid formula, which does not conceal its approval of the abuse of police power. (Andersen, 1994: 13)

This is perhaps the clearest example of the blurring of the lines between fact and fiction. The heroic cop is justified in bending the rules in the fictional world of the police drama. Corruption in a noble cause allows him or her to continue fighting to clean the streets of crime and protect the public. When we shift to fact-based entertainment – the more nebulous realm of the reality police show – the audience is presented with similar but less grand examples of rules being broken. In adopting the tone of police fiction, the media conspire in such rule-breaking, enabling transgressions of the law to be justified in the same way they are in police drama – namely the villain is caught, justice is done and the public are served:

> *Cops* unites portrayals of state-sanctioned violence and a highly effective law enforcement agency – whereby violence against suspects symbolically reinforces the social power and status of the official institution. (Fishman, 1999: 281)

The public, however, are not served. Suspects' rights are eroded, cheered on by the reality cop show. It is not only the erosion of due process, witnessed by cameras and explained away by programme-makers as a necessity of justice, that is problematic, but the media's loss of independence in moving from an observer to an active protagonist in these shows. As Andersen's US drug policy example illustrates, this 'post-documentary' (Corner, 2000) form may be influencing criminal justice policy and shaping police practice.

Appeal and voyeurism

The growth of reality television can be explained on one level by its popularity. It is the case in all forms of entertainment that a successful film, documentary or drama will be copied. So this begs the question, what is the appeal of programmes like *Police, Camera, Action* and *Cops*? Hoggart (1998) identifies three reasons for the enjoyment in watching such programmes. First, there is 'the schoolchild's peculiar delight in seeing someone else get into trouble' (Hoggart, 1998: 2). This is perhaps a variation on laughing at someone else's misfortune, the person who falls over in the street, for example. Nevertheless, this has perhaps a more disturbing overtone. The likes of *Beadle's About* and *You've Been Framed* in which mishaps captured on home video are broadcast as entertainment remove the consequences of people's injuries from the act itself. Similarly, the appeal of watching the spectacular car crash and the dangerous driver arrested are stripped of their context and never balanced by concern for the party involved. It is the spectacle that is all important.

We can perhaps consider this use of CCTV and police camera footage as an extension of a spectacle of punishment: the public's desire to see justice being done. This has parallels with the development of public punishment, what Foucault terms the 'the theatrical representation of pain' (Foucault, 1979: 14) which had been a crucial element in state justice until the birth of the prison. From Roman times, publicity and spectacle were an important element in punishment with gladiatorial battles and Christians thrown to the lions in the vast public arenas. This continued with the extensive use of pillories and stocks, hangings and beheading for treason, one of the most spectacular examples being the execution of Charles I:

> The masked executioner raised the axe which was to cut through his sovereign's neck, and a moment afterwards turned to the excited crowd and said 'Behold the head of a traitor'. (Pike, 1968: 167)

The function of public punishment went beyond the simplicity of making an example of the condemned. Foucault (1979) identifies several other purposes for public forms of punishment. Along with the control over the body, the reason for such extreme visible torture was the reinforcement of the power of the state over its subjects. At the crucial moment of execution, the political might of the state was displayed for all to see – 'the physical strength of the sovereign beating down upon the body of his adversary and mastering it' (Foucault, 1979: 49). A breach of the law was a personal attack on the king, who responded with extreme violence, and 'the affront was righted' (Dreyfuss and Rabinow, 1982: 145).

However, such terrifying rituals required the public to watch, for without them much of the effect was lost:

> Not only must people know, they must see with their own eyes. Because they must be made to be afraid; but also because they must be the witnesses, the guarantors, of the punishment, and because they must to a certain extent take part in it. (Foucault, 1979: 58)

Foucault's (1979) account of the development of the prison replaces 'the *mise-en-scène* of the public execution' (Sparks, 1992: 34) with a process of correction carried out in secret. However, as Sparks contends, such an account of modern penality 'tended to neglect the survival of the demand for retribution in modern culture' (Sparks, 1992: 34). A version of the spectacle, which Foucault argues disappeared with the birth of the prison, 'persists vigorously' (Sparks, 1992: 55) in televisual and cinematic representations of crime and punishment. He cites two aspects of crime and punishment in the mass media: first, vigilante characters such as Clint Eastwood's 'Dirty Harry' and the *Death Wish* films with Charles Bronson. These, he argues are moral tales with 'immense public salience' (Sparks, 1992: 35). A parallel exists here between monarchic power over the body of the wrongdoer described by Foucault with the revenge killings of Eastwood and Bronson: the gallows and guillotine replaced by the .44 Magnum.

It is possible to place reality police shows in this bracket too. The arrest of the perpetrator of some street crime is, for the television audience, justice in action: the might of the law brought to bear. A lack of audience research precludes any definite correlation between the appeal of the reality police show and an audience's desire for justice to be done. However, it seems likely that at least part of the attraction of such shows is similar to that of the baying crowds at the gallows.

Hoggart's second and third reasons for the appeal and consequent proliferation of reality police shows also relate to the spectacle of justice and the power of the watcher. He argues that the audience witnessing the arrest of the suspect, the reckless driver caught on camera and subsequently punished, offers the audience justice in action. We have seen how the good have triumphed in fiction, and noted the volume of police success stories in the tabloid press: infotainment and faction are no different. The reassuring message that the police win the battle against crime on the streets is a mantra chanted just as loudly by the likes of *Police, Camera, Action!* as it was by *Dixon of Dock Green* and *The Bill.*

Hoggart's third point concerns the power of watching what we were not intended to see. This notion of surveillance and voyeurism requires more detailed discussion.

Panoptics and reality television

Perhaps ironically the audience, once such a vital component of capital punishment, was one factor that led to the disappearance of punishment as a spectacle. Public executions had been the symbol of monarchic power but such order over the masses often disintegrated into mass disorder:

> ...power was perceived to be flowing out of the hands of the punishing authority and into the dangerously unstable reservoir of the great crowds. (Nellis and Hale, 1982: 53)

Although it is unclear when exactly the prison became the principal punitive measure, Foucault (1979) identifies a development in attitudes towards discipline, describing what he calls 'normalisation' – 'concerned to induce conformity rather than to exact retribution' (Garland, 1990: 145). Central to assessing standards of non-conformity was surveillance:

> An apparatus in which the techniques that make it possible to see induce effects of power, and in which, conversely, the means of coercion make those on whom they are applied clearly visible. (Foucault, 1979: 171)

The continuous gaze of authority would control individuals allowing for the process of normalising deviance to occur.

> The building circular – A cage, glazed – a glass lantern about the size of *Ranleigh* – The prisoners in their cells, occupying the circum-ference – The officers in the centre. By blinds and other contrivances, the inspectors concealed...from the observation of the prisoners: hence the sentiment of a sort of omnipresence – The whole circuit reviewable with little, or if necessary without any, change of place. One station in the inspection part affording the most perfect view of every cell. (Bentham, 1798, in Evans, 1982: 20)

Bentham's Panopticon, described above, was the embodiment of just such a system of surveillance leading to, as Foucault (1979) saw it, a system of self-regulation. Inmates unable to detect whether they were under the watchful eye of the supervisor could not risk escape or violence: 'visibility is a trap' (Foucault, 1979: 200). This was in marked contrast to the gallows where to exact monarchical power it was necessary to have a crowd, violence, the army, the clergy and so on. In Bentham's Panopticon a gaze was all that was required: the role of the monarch was replaced with a machine in which no one person was entrusted with power:

> In the Panopticon each person, depending on his place, is watched by all or certain of the others. (Gordon, 1980: 158)

The role of the Panopticon in the development of the prison was seen as crucial by Foucault. He argues that panopticism, a system of generalised surveillance, became the general form of discipline and power in the eighteenth century – in schools, the army, factories and hospitals.

Although Foucault did not extend his discussions of panopticism to modern surveillance technology, others have.[2] The rise of CCTV and police cameras, it is argued, contain panoptic elements. Writers such as Gandy (1989) and Gordon (1986) have suggested that modern surveillance constitutes an 'electronic panopticon' in which the CCTV cameras in city centres and computer databases of personal information create an invisible gaze across all aspects of our lives. Poster (1997) argues there now exists a 'superpanopticon' in which the interdependency of computer databases create what Haggerty and Ericson describe as a 'data double' of ourselves (Haggerty and Ericson, 2000: 625). These allow government agencies and big business to trace behavioural patterns and trends through analysis of our data doubles, shorn of all unnecessary personality traits.

Mathiesen (1997) has used the term 'synopticon' to indicate a sharing of public images – everybody is watching everybody else. Haggerty and Ericson (2000) point out that 'the monitoring of the powerful has been eased by the proliferation of relatively inexpensive video cameras'. The human rights pressure group Witness issues people with such cameras in order to film human rights abuses. In July 2001 in Britain a student captured on his video camera two police officers beating a suspect (*The Guardian*, 25 July 2001). The synoptic power of the public was very visible at the anti-capitalism demonstrations at Genoa in July 2001 where Italian police were seen beating peaceful protestors with batons (*The Guardian*, 27 July 2001). Furthermore, CCTV camera filmed two police officers in England beating a suspect on a deserted street. PCs Barry Vardon and

Steve Watson were convicted of assault and sentenced to three months in prison (*The Independent*, 12 December 2000).

Are we perhaps seeing the reversal of the panoptic power the police can exert through the use of CCTV, replaced with the synoptic power of the video camera? One can foresee the reality television show that follows protestors as they are mistreated by the police, or the video diary of the suspect beaten up by police.

The panoptic and synoptic both induce a further development. That of a desire to be watched. Whereas Bentham's Panopticon was designed for power over the individual, inducing fear and conformity, in the twenty-first century, to be watched provokes a positive as well as a negative response. This development in the use of CCTV for entertainment purposes suggests that surveillance in the twenty-first century is as much about entertainment as it is about control. The architect of a New York restaurant that incorporates CCTV as part of its design argues that 'yesterday we were nervous that we were being watched. Today we're nervous that we're not being watched' (Elizabeth Diller, in *A History of Surveillance*, Channel 4, 12 August 2001). Young offenders caught with video tapes of their crimes argue that without recording it, it's as if it hadn't taken place: 'increasingly to be surveilled is to be. I am surveilled therefore I am' (Mark Pesce, in *A History of Surveillance*, Channel 4, 12 August 2001). This exhibitionism is, in part perhaps, a response to the ubiquity of surveillance: an opportunity to reflect back on the watcher and take some control back. One thing that reality television has shown is that we are a nation not only of voyeurs but also of exhibitionists. The contestants on the likes of *Big Brother* are there in the vain hope of being spotted for a future of never-ending fame and fortune; the characters in docu-soaps likewise. When Emma, a shop assistant on a make-up counter in *Lakesiders* talked to camera about discovering her fiancé's affair with her sister, she later said that her participation in the programme was less cathartic and more opportunistic, as she hoped the programme would help launch her singing career.

Is this what we see with reality police television? Does this make the police exhibitionists? We have already seen how the police carefully manage their image but we have also seen how unreal reality television is. Greer points out: '…it is always the case that although people who volunteer for reality show may be exhibitionists, someone who is careful to remain unwatched is pulling their strings' (Greer, 2001: 1). Two observations can be made here. First, we have seen how the police shape their image and have become more media-aware in recent times. If we accept the rise of the synoptic, the inevitable surveillance of the surveillor, then the police are surely bound to attempt to mould their image and increase the opportunity for positive messages about their work. The desire to be observed is related to the rise in celebrity – this drives the *Big Brother* contestants far more than the comparatively measly £70,000 prize money. Are we witnessing the development of the celebrity cop to new status? Is this, in part, a reaction to the increase in crime drama and the consequent rise in the celebrity status of the fictional cop?

A further development in the rise of police infotainment has been the use of official police interviews used as entertainment. In October 2001, Channel Five broadcast the police interviews with Fred West, accused of killing 12 women before committing suicide in prison on 1 January 1995. The programme makers, Portman Entertainment, justify the programme on the grounds that it raised the question of more victims that have remained undiscovered. This suggests a further potential influence of the media over police practice. If interviewing officers are aware that the video tape of the interview may eventually end up on television, this may affect their behaviour. It may also act as a form of surveillance in that the police's actions during interview will be subject to scrutiny. May we get to a point where interviews are rehearsed and changed to make them more televisual?

A further development occurred recently with the releasing of police interviews to the press by Christine and Neil Hamilton. Their decision was allegedly based on their desire to clear their name, having been accused of committing a sexual assault on a woman in a flat in Ilford on 5 May 2001.

Notes

1 *The Independent on Sunday* reported on 19 August 2001 that five of the largest Hollywood studios have announced a pay-per-view online Internet video system.
2 For an interesting discussion on panopticism and modern surveillance see Lyon (1993, 2001), Norris and Armstrong (1999) and Haggerty and Ericson (2000).
3 The BCS reported that 66 per cent of people thought crime had risen between 1997 and 1999 despite an overall fall of 10 per cent; also 36 per cent of women do not go out at night alone due to fear of crime.

Chapter 8

Trial by media – courting contempt

Introduction

Throughout this book, we have been discussing how important and complex the relationships between the police and the media are in fact and in fiction. Prominent themes already reviewed have concerned the ways in which the media refract realities and mediate messages about policing, including those that the police themselves seek to promote. We considered in Chapter 7 some issues and dangers associated with the further blurring of the lines between fact and fiction in the plethora of 'factional' programmes now commonly referred to as 'infotainment', many of which focus directly or indirectly on the work and workings of the public police. In the 'synoptic society', the many now watch the few (Matthiesen, 1997), and the omnipresence of CCTV cameras in city centres and shopping malls, for example, ensures a bountiful supply of footage which can be readily recycled for informational and entertainment purposes in both factual and factional programmes. In the risk society, cameras are becoming lighter, less obtrusive and ubiquitous, monitoring motorways, watching workers and workplaces, guarding 'gated communities', functioning as flies on the wall at dawn raid ridealongs and inside police interview rooms. Thus far, in Britain at least, one arena of policework has escaped the systematic gaze of the camera, in factual programming and to a significant – if lesser – extent in fictional police drama. That locus is the courtroom where the modern spectacle of justice is played out in the context of the adversarial trial. In this chapter we examine the media's impact on the reporting of court cases and consider the consequences not only for the police in bringing successful prosecutions, but also in terms of the course of due process of justice. We begin by reviewing controversies concerning payments to witnesses in high-profile cases, and then outline ongoing debates about the introduction of cameras into Britain's courts, making reference to experience in the United States, where cameras seem to have become almost as much a feature of courtroom fixtures and fittings as the judge's high-backed chair. We go on to speculate as to the possible implications for the police of electronic broadcast coverage of court proceedings, something that may well become a reality in the not too distant future. As we shall suggest, recent developments in police training for officers giving evidence in court could not be more timely. Furthermore, questions that arise from the media's existing intrusions into court cases could be further magnified should those proceedings be televised or broadcast on the Internet.

Rough justice or storm in a chequebook?

As we have already seen, a recurring concern for those who subscribe to what Reiner (1997, 2000b) tags the view of media as 'subversive' is its potential role in undermining due process of law. Publicity surrounding the case of O. J. Simpson in the USA and in Britain that of Fred and Rosemary West, for example, has heightened concerns that the 'golden thread' of defendants being innocent until proven guilty is being seriously compromised by press coverage of unfolding crime investigations and, in particular, because of payments to witnesses. Grave misgivings about the way in which the West case had been reported led Tony Butler, the then Chief Constable of Gloucester, to complain formally to the Attorney-General and warn the media that any possible breaches of the Contempt of Court Act 1981 would be reported (*The Guardian*, 3 January 1995). Of particular concern at that time, were allegations that a serving police officer had been seeking to negotiate a deal for the inside story of the Cromwell Street investigation (Innes, 1999: 274). As discussed in Chapter 7, the *Sunday Mirror* newspaper was found guilty of contempt in publishing an interview which led to the abandonment of the first trial of two Leeds United footballers on assault charges against an Asian youth. The interview with the victim's father had been published at the time when the jury was considering their verdict, leading the judge to order a retrial at an estimated cost to the taxpayer of £8 million (BBC Online, 5 March 2002).

Even the most punctilious use of quotation marks and of the word 'alleged' in relation to suspects can fray that golden thread of due process, conveying to readers – who may include among them potential and actual jurors – strong impressions of guilt, long before any charges have been preferred, if indeed they ever are. This, of course, presents issues for the police in the way that they circumnavigate what Morgan, a Grampian Police superintendent refers to as 'the pitfalls of pre-trial briefings' (1998: 47). The problems surrounding this area are closely linked to the reliance of the media on the police as primary news sources. It is a relationship that many regard as 'collusive', involving the police, as it often does, in the provision of so-called deep background and off-the-record commentary, which might controversially include sharing or enhancing suspicions about (not yet charged) individuals close to the victim of a serious crime (Innes, 1999: 277). On occasions, the resultant coverage can be tantamount to 'trial by the media' and, a decade ago, Jolyon Jenkins was prescient in suggesting that a courtroom reckoning was inevitable:

> Sooner or later, a defence barrister will successfully argue in court that his or her client cannot get a fair trial because of the advance publicity, and the judge will throw the case out. It will be most salutary. The police will have to think twice about feeding juicy titbits to their friends in the tabloid press, for fear that they will fail to get a conviction. This will be an altogether more satisfactory solution than trying to prosecute journalists. (Jenkins, 1993: 3)

As we have seen in Chapter 3, proactive police–media relations policies are no longer an adjunct to police operations, but have increasingly become an integral part of serious criminal investigations. A central purpose of modern media management strategy has been to limit the potential for journalists to 'contaminate' witnesses through offering them inducements to 'sell and tell' their stories (Innes, 1999: 274; 2001: 42). The issue of 'chequebook journalism' has been a bone of contention at least since 1966 when reports emerged of weekly payments to the chief prosecution witness in the Myra Hindley and Ian Brady murder trials. In 1979, the Jeremy Thorpe trial for conspiracy to murder was shrouded in controversy when it was revealed that key prosecution witness Peter Bessell was to receive a 'bonus' fee from the *Sunday Telegraph* if Thorpe were eventually convicted (Berlins, 1997).

From the Moors Murderers case onwards, successive Attorneys-General have considered proposals for legislative measures to curb the practice of chequebook journalism (Higham, 2002). Speaking at a conference of European Chief Justices and Attorneys-General in 1996, the then Attorney-General Sir Nicholas Lyell warned of the possible threats to justice:

> By signing a contract with a newspaper, a witness may have the incentive to exaggerate. Even if a witness is not swayed by selling his story to the media, there can be damaging suggestions, under cross-examination, that the evidence may be flawed and the credibility of a truthful witness may be undermined. (In Higham, 2002)

In March 2002, the Lord Chancellors' Department published a Consultation Paper outlining the government's proposals to make it a criminal offence to pay witnesses in criminal proceedings (Lord Chancellor's Department, 2002). This proposal sought to make it a criminal offence: 'to make or receive payments or enter into agreements to make or receive payments to, or by, witnesses' (Lord Chancellor's Department, 2002: 5) which would carry a maximum sentence of two years' imprisonment and an unlimited fine. These steps were in response to recent high-profile criminal cases such as Rosemary West in 1995 and Paul Gadd in 1999.

In the West case, five prosecution witnesses had been paid sums by newspapers of between £750 and £30,000. The Court of Appeal, when reviewing the convictions of Rose West, thought that the whole issue of media payments to witnesses needed to be revisited stating that 'We believe that in some circumstances it could put justice at risk' (*The Guardian*, 25 February 2002). In November 1999, Paul Gadd, better known as Gary Glitter, was acquitted of having sex with a minor, Ms Alison Brown, in 1987. The court had been told that Brown had already received £5,000 for a story about her relationship with him from the *News of the World* newspaper in 1987. After Gadd was arrested for possessing child pornography in November 1997, Brown signed a further contract with the *News of the World* under which she would receive £10,000 on publication of a story and a further £25,000 on the publication of a second story should Gadd be convicted. The trial judge, Mr Justice Butterfield, expressed the view that the pay-out by the *News of the World* was 'highly reprehensible' adding that: 'It is not illegal but it is to be greatly deprecated' (BBC Online, 12 November 1999).

Since the publication of the Consultation Paper there have been further cases in which witness payments have been said to affect the trial outcome. Amy Gehring, a biology teacher, was cleared of four counts of indecent assault on two teenage boys in February 2002. One of the boys admitted to a deal with *The Sunday People* and *The Mail on Sunday* worth

£10,000 (Dyer, 2002). The Consultation Paper suggests that 'the ultimate mischief' that arises from making payments to witnesses is a miscarriage of justice that can come about in a number of ways:

- the payment directly influences the witness testimony – they may leave something out to create an exclusive story or exaggerate to increase their worth;

- payment may undermine the credibility of a witness;

- the interview with a journalist may make the witness lose objectivity with sensational elements brought out by the journalist leading to a misleading and unbalanced account in court.

However, there are commentators who suggest that five notorious cases in 35 years hardly constitutes a major problem and that this whole issue is a mere 'storm in a chequebook' (Greenslade, 2002). Lord Wakeham writing in the *News of the World* (Wakeham, 1999) considered the Gary Glitter trial to be one such example. He suggests that not only are the incidences of witness payments affecting trials rare, but that there has never been any substantial evidence to support such claims. He submits that in some cases witness payments may lead to a conviction: 'In the trial of Rose West, a large number of witnesses approached newspapers in the first place – who, in truth, helped unearth evidence of use to the police' (Wakeham, 1999: 8).

Berlins is also unconvinced by the 'image evoked of greedy witnesses telling big lies for big money and thereby distorting the course of justice' (Berlins, 1999: 17). For obvious reasons, there is little scope for undertaking systematic research on 'effects' on juries, who remain inaccessible to effects researchers owing to s.8, Contempt of Court Act 1981 which protects the secrecy of jury room deliberations. Berlins rightly draws attention to the paradox whereby prejudicial pre-trial publicity by the media rarely results in contempt of court proceedings, while the issue of payments to witnesses attracts such opprobrium. He also notes, as we have discussed in Chapter 7, that the legal establishment has traditionally placed much faith in the 'good sense' of juries not to be affected by the former, but seems reluctant to trust that insight in respect of the latter. The Press Complaints Commission's Acting Chairman, Professor Robert Pinker, pointed out that that strict guidelines already govern situations when newspapers offer money for stories. He argues that the Lord Chancellor's Consultation Paper is 'a futile gesture to deal with a largely illusory problem' (*Today*, BBC Radio Four, 2 May 2002). Interestingly, he stated that the government's plans made a 'breathtakingly slender and illogical' distinction between payments by the police for information and payments by newspapers, without explaining 'why a police informant should not exaggerate information because he or she is being paid' (*Today*, BBC Radio Four, 2 May 2002). In a real sense, concerns about payments to potential witnesses do extend to the police themselves, a point forcefully made by the executive director of the Society of Authors, Bob Satchwell, who, like Professor Pinker, has reservations about plans to outlaw payments to witnesses:

> The offer of rewards for information leading to a conviction has long been an effective aid to justice, usually with the active encourage-ment of the police. Does this mean rewards, part of justice since history began, are to be abandoned? (BBC Online, 5 March 2002)

As Innes (2000) has commented, in recent years there has been a discernible 'professionalisation' of the role of the police informant, manifested by the spread of rewards schemes which extend far beyond the traditional payment of gratuities to low-level 'copper's narks' for 'information received'. While police use of informants fits in very much with the ethos of 'intelligence-led policing' and has been praised by the Audit Commission (1993) as a cost-effective means of solving crime, there are many difficult moral and ethical dilemmas surrounding this area. Indeed, Norris and Dunnighan (2000) have demonstrated how a lack of clarity and consistency in the way that the police handle informers can lead to various forms of conflict, and how potentially the use of in-formants can have an undermining influence on subsequent court cases.

The 'professionalisation' of the informant is evidenced by develop-ments such as *Crimestoppers* (Button, 2002; Ericson and Haggerty, 1997) and by the expansion of witness protection programmes, the latter sometimes involving significant police-sanctioned payments and induce-ments. These extremely controversial cases often involve witness intimidation and so-called 'supergrasses', whose testimony might be 'traded' for immunity from prosecution and a complete change of identity and relocation. In their research in Strathclyde, Fyfe and McKay (2000) detected concerns among prosecutors about payments and protection given to witnesses. Although defence lawyers might regard it to be a 'barrel-scraping tactic', procurators-fiscal still recognised that protection and relocation could be used to raise doubts about the recipient's credibility as a witness (Fyfe and McKay, 2000: 291). Payments to a subsequently discredited witness in the Damilola Taylor trial of 2002 provoked widespread debate in England and Wales about whether or not offering rewards for witnesses to come forward and testify is in the best interests of justice. Indeed, many are worried that the proliferation of a 'rewards for information' culture could result in witnesses being less prepared to come forward as a matter of public duty while becoming more likely to be motivated by personal profit. Innes is surely right to sound an admonitory note about the possible damage to the police image and legitimacy that might accrue from ever more formalised arrangements with informants, some of whom, after all, may ultimately be required to give evidence in court:

> In the light of a number of serious miscarriages of justice, the police are no longer unquestioningly accepted as a bastion of social order. Under such conditions, the question remains as to whether it is acceptable for the police to seek to develop and formalise the relationship with informants, in the fashion that is being followed. (2000: 382)

Again, as we suggested in Chapter 3, in respectively pursuing the prosecution case and the exclusive inside story, the police and the media may perhaps share more similarities in this murky area than is often acknowledged. The problems of contempt of court associated with payments for witnesses and informants could well be exacerbated for both by the development of electronic broadcasting of court proceedings, to which we now turn our attention.

Court *in camera* or cameras in court?

The increased use of television in courtroom proceedings over recent years strongly suggests the likelihood of major changes occurring in the nature and extent of media involvement in the legal process during the twenty-first century. The arguments supporting and denouncing the use of cameras in court have been well documented in recent years by disputed media reporting of the trials of O. J. Simpson in 1995 (*People of the State of California* v. *Orenthal James Simpson*, 4 October 1995) and Louise Woodward in 1997 (*The Commonwealth of Massachusetts* v. *Louise Woodward*, 6 October 1997) (Luft, 1997; Trigobov, 1997; Brill, 1996; Lassiter, 1996 and Goldfarb, 1995). Trials such as these have led to accusations of justice being reduced to voyeuristic entertainment (Altheide, 1984; Barber, 1983; and Clark, 1994) while others argue that justice should be seen to be done (Burgi, 1995; Denniston, 1994; and Hernandez, 1996). The principal arguments of both sides are summarised in Table 8.1.

The presence of cameras in courtrooms can be traced back to the

Table 8.1   Electronic broadcasting of courtroom proceedings

Arguments in favour	Arguments against
Scrutiny and transparency of the legal process	Fosters disrespect for the court and other justice agencies (including the police)
Education – informs the public of the workings of the law, police and the courts	Television distorts and sensationalises the trial process
Some research suggests court participants not affected by cameras	Some research suggests court participants are affected by cameras
O. J. Simpson trial the exception that proves the rule	Witnesses and victims less likely to testify
Case law supports the use of cameras in court	Case law supports the ban of cameras in court

United States trial in Flemington, New Jersey of Bruno Hauptmann (*State v. Hauptmann*, 80 L.Ed. 461, 1935) who was charged with the kidnap and murder of famous aviator Charles Lindbergh's baby son. The courtroom was said to contain '141 newspaper reporters and photographers; 125 telegraph operators; and 40 messengers' (Stepniak, 1998: 35). The trial led to the American Bar Association House of Delegates issuing Canon 35 of the *American Bar Association's Canons of Professional and Judicial Ethics*, recommending that photographers be barred from courtrooms.

In the United Kingdom, photography was also prohibited by s.41, Criminal Justice Act 1925. The ban on photographic equipment in the courts of England and Wales was extended to television cameras by *Re Barber* v. *Lloyds Underwriters* (1987, 1 QB 103). As parts of Europe began experimenting with electronic broadcasting of legal proceedings, the Bar Council of England and Wales compiled a report on the use of cameras in courtrooms around the world (Caplan, 1989). The report recommended the limited use of television cameras under strict regulation for an experimental period of two years. However, the recommendations were never implemented.

The most significant development came in 1991 when the BBC broadcast the first televised trial in Britain. *The Trial* was a five-part series showing footage from criminal trials in Scottish courts but it was pre-recorded and not broadcast live (Hogan and Mason, 1999). It was the result of strict legal guidelines allowing media access to the Scottish courts announced in 1992 by Lord Hope of Craighead, then Lord President of the Scottish judiciary (Hope, 1994). The practice directions were specifically designed to encourage documentary and educational programmes. These stated that the Scottish Judiciary would allow 'the use of TV in other cases where there would be no risk to the administration of justice' (Hope, 1994: para. b).

The Hope Guidelines for the use of cameras in Scottish courts allowed for the possibility of the Lockerbie trial to be televised. The trial took place on 'neutral' ground at Camp Zeist in the Netherlands under Scots law on 3 May 2000. The BBC, with the support of the major American networks, sought permission from the High Court in Edinburgh to broadcast the trial gavel to gavel on the Internet and provide extracts for television. Their request was rejected by Lord McFadyen who ruled that broadcasting the trial could have a detrimental effect on both witnesses and the administration of justice. The BBC appealed, arguing that Lord McFadyen's ruling breached the European Convention on Human Rights by restricting the freedom of the press under Article 10. On 20 April 2001, the Edinburgh High Court, in dismissing the appeal, ruled that under Article 6 of the ECHR the right to a fair trial should be protected.

The subsequent appeal of Abdelbaset Ali Mohmed Al Megrahi (who was found guilty of the Lockerbie bombing in January 2001) was also held at Camp Zeist in January 2002. However, this time the BBC was granted the right to broadcast the appeal by the Scottish Lord Justice-General, Lord Cullen. The recorded broadcast was shown on Scottish Television, but the appeal was transmitted live and unedited on the BBC's website, BBC Online.

Alongside the developments of the Lockerbie trial broadcast have been the decisions to allow cameras in public inquiries. Significant developments here have been CNN's successful application to film parts of the Shipman Inquiry (Shipman Inquiry, 2001) into the medical career of Dr Harold Shipman, convicted of the murders of 15 patients in 2000, the Bristol Royal Infirmary children's heart surgery inquiry (Kennedy, 2001) and the Southall Rail crash inquiry (Huff, 2000). Furthermore, in December 2000 the Lord Chancellor, Lord Irvine, suggested that cameras could be allowed to film high-profile appeal cases. He argued that televising such cases might have 'a valuable educative effect' by giving the public a 'better understanding about the nature of the judicial system' (*The Guardian*, 24 January 2001: 1).

The increase in the use of electronic broadcast coverage of court proceedings and the development of broadband coverage of cases on the Internet could have significant consequences for police testimony and, by extension, on public perceptions of police integrity and effectiveness, perceptions that, as we have seen in Chapter 3, police image workers have been assiduous in presenting in a positive light. Stockdale and Gresham's report on police testimony in court suggested that a quarter of police officers actively disliked giving evidence, 'finding it a nerve-racking experience and often saying that they "hated" or "detested" going into the witness box' (Stockdale and Gresham, 1995: 4). Although any assessment of the impact of cameras in court on British police officers can only be, for the most part, speculative at this stage, the case of Mark Fuhrman in the O. J. Simpson trial in the USA provides a useful case study on the possible effects of televising court cases in which officers give evidence.

Officer and a gentle man? The case of Mark Fuhrman

Lassiter (1996) terms television's effect on trials 'the comprehensive and instantaneous feedback loop'. He argues that the nature of television coverage of court cases is qualitatively different from that of the press and suggests that the broadcast of trials 'live and as it happens' allows for a 'two-way street' between public and proceedings. He suggests that television also allows for expert commentary on each day of the trial as well as affording the opportunity for national public opinion polls on the case to function as a kind of 'shadow jury':

> By virtue of re-broadcast and nightly analysis, the combination of television media in and out of the courtroom provides a feedback loop, which permits the judge, lawyers, witnesses, and jurors at trial to become aware of the public reaction to what goes on at trial – also virtually instantaneously. (Lassiter, 1996: 1010)

Lassiter's arguments and the broader implications for police officers giving evidence in televised trials are illustrated by the testimony of Los Angeles police officer Mark Fuhrman during the O. J. Simpson trial in 1995.

Mark Fuhrman was a detective with the Los Angeles Police Department, West Los Angeles Homicide Division. Fuhrman allegedly found a glove covered in blood which matched another glove found at the house of the victim, Nicole Brown Simpson. Simpson's defence attorney, F. Lee Bailey, sought to portray Fuhrman as a racist officer who had planted the glove at the defendant's house in order to further his own police career. Furthermore, the defence suggested that they were able to produce a witness who had heard Fuhrman make racist remarks. The witness,

Kathleen Bell, worked above a Marine recruiting station where Fuhrman sought to enlist, and it was here, she stated, that she had heard him utter racist comments. Bell only came to the fore as a witness against Fuhrman because she had seen him on the television coverage of the preliminary trial. In her own television appearance on the *Larry King Live* show (CNN, 30 January 1995), Bell admitted that she would not have known who Fuhrman was and could not have come forward had she not seen him on the broadcast coverage of the preliminary hearing.

To discredit Fuhrman further, the defence stated they had a second witness, Marine Sergeant Max Cordoba, who would testify Fuhrman had called him 'a nigger'. That evening, the ABC network aired an interview with Cordoba in which he stated he had never spoken to the defence team about appearing as a witness. The following night on NBC, a further interview appeared in which Cordoba said he remembered speaking to the defence team. Lassiter argues that 'the media stampeded the trial process' (Lassiter, 1997: 1012) in generating the witness testimony of Kathy Bell against Fuhrman and in damaging the credibility of Max Cordoba to such an extent he was never called as a witness by Simpson's defence team.

Fuhrman himself was publicly humiliated on national television as jurors heard a tape recording of an interview with professor and screen-writer Laura McKinny. Speaking on the subject of the effectiveness of female police officers, Fuhrman said, 'They don't do anything. They don't go out and initiate contact with some 6'5" nigger that's been in prison for seven years pumping weights' (Trial Transcript, *People of the State of California* v. *Orenthal James Simpson*, Week 33, 5 September 1995). Fuhrman used the word 'nigger' 42 times in the interview. Several more witnesses were produced testifying that Fuhrman had made racist comments towards them. On further cross-examination Fuhrman invoked his Fifth Amendment right and refused to answer questions relating to the planting of the bloody glove on the Simpson estate. His credibility as a witness was fatally undermined, having previously sworn on oath that he had not used the word 'nigger' in the previous ten years.

The testimony of Mark Fuhrman in the O. J. Simpson case and the subsequent discrediting of him as a witness illustrates two important points arising from this discussion of police testimony in televised court-rooms: first, Lassiter's 'instantaneous feedback loop' where television coverage of the trial and the consequent analysis and audience inter-action can potentially alter the course of the trial process; second, the broadcasting of trials places even further pressure on police officers, who are already stressed about giving evidence. Let us consider what televised trials might mean for the British police.

Camera-ready coppers?

In 1995, the Home Office Police Research Group produced a report examining the performance of police officers in the witness box in the Magistrates' and High Courts (Stockdale and Gresham, 1995). This was in response to concerns that the quality of police evidence may have been adversely affecting the outcome of trials:

> The way in which evidence is presented and the impression given by officers have the capacity to affect the perceptions of judges, magistrates, jurors and others present and hence the credence they place on police evidence. Clarity of presentation and performance under cross-examination have significant roles to play in establishing the adequacy and integrity of police evidence. (Stockdale and Gresham, 1995: 1)

The report concluded that officers' performance is 'generally satisfactory but variable' (Stockdale and Gresham, 1995: v). Criticisms of officers included over-reliance on notebooks, insufficient case preparation, poor presentational skills and an overconfident or aggressive manner under cross-examination. The report made a number of recommendations, including the production of a training video which highlighted good and bad practice in the presentation of police evidence in court.

In 2001, the Metropolitan Police's Professional Standards – Civil Actions Investigations Unit (CAIU) in conjunction with John Beggs Training produced a training video called *Officer Safety in the Witness Box* (Mulraney, 2001a: 27). The hour-long video, which is to be shown to 'every operational officer in the force' (Mulraney, 2001a: 27), featured experienced barristers and police officers discussing various aspects of giving evidence and cross-examination in court. Ronald Thwaites QC, an experienced defence counsel, commented on the video:

> The main failing of the police is they don't understand that it's all about making a good impression…I think that many of them tend to take some of the behavioural traits they've adopted out on the street into the witness box; in particular, a certain arrogance which comes with wearing the blue uniform and I think they need to jettison that attitude when they enter the witness box.

Inspector Martin Bruton of the CIAU noted that the video should address some of the failings identified by the Stockdale and Gresham report:

> Barristers have been using the same techniques for years...but for some reason the service has not caught onto these techniques. This is the first time that barristers have been totally candid and open in what they do. (Cited in Mulraney, 2001a: 27)

The performance of officers in court is likely to come under increasing scrutiny as the development of electronic broadcasting of court proceedings continues. There has been some research on what effect, if any, the presence of cameras has on courtroom participants. Several significant reports based on pilot studies and experiments on cameras in courtrooms have come up with a variety of conclusions. One of the problems in this kind of research (as indeed with the media effects studies discussed in Chapter 2) is one of method as West (1997) notes:

> No matter how many social scientists dance their methodological tango, there is no valid way to demonstrate that television in the court does or does not affect the way the drama unfolds. (West, 1997: 48)

It is extremely difficult to isolate and measure the influence of cameras on behaviour (Stepniak, 1998). Researchers tend to rely on self-reporting by court participants and perceptions of them by observers and others present in the court. The difficulty which arises here is how accurate such perceptions are and how likely it is that legal professionals would admit to being perturbed by the presence of cameras:

> Since judges are supposed to be impartial...it is possible that those who believed themselves compromised by the improper influence of television coverage might be disinclined to acknowledge their partiality. (Lassiter, 1996: 994)

Those in favour of cameras can point to several studies that show cameras have almost no effect on proceedings. Research by Kassin (1984) and Borgida *et al.* (1990) used dummy trials and shadow juries to establish the effect of a camera on witnesses and jurors and both reported minimal detrimental effect. Several states in the US have conducted their own research into the effects of cameras in their courts (California – Short, 1981; State of Nevada, 1980; State of Arizona, 1980; State of New Jersey, 1994). All four states were unanimous in their results: the presence of cameras in the court had few side-effects on the trial or its participants. The Judicial Conference of the United States also reported on its three-year experiment of allowing cameras in six federal district courts and two circuit courts (Johnson 1993). It concluded that there had been no negative impact on the trials.

However, there are also several reports which suggest that electronic media coverage of court proceedings may have detrimental effects on court participants. In 1991 the New York Bar Association reported that cameras do have a prejudicial impact (Jaffe, 1991). Among the findings, 35 per cent of all attorneys said that the atmosphere was uneasy as a result of cameras, 56 per cent of defence attorneys reported that they felt the fairness of the trial was affected by cameras and 19 per cent of witnesses admitted to being distracted. Some studies from the United States also suggest that the presence of cameras in court has a significant impact on the behaviour of court participants. In New York, the State Committee found that:

> What is very much alive are the concerns about the psychological impact of the camera: how will the realization that their every word or gesture is being transmitted to a vast, unseen audience affect the behavior of trial participants? (New York State Committee, 1997: Exhibit 1)

The most recent report on this area by Mason (2000) sums up the mixed findings of the reports on cameras in court. Reporting on the effect of electronic broadcast equipment on court participants at the International Criminal Tribunal for the former Yugoslavia (ICTY), his findings suggest that while respondents self-reported cameras had little or no effect on their own behaviour in court, there were some who felt that cameras did affect proceedings. Significantly, the report suggests that those who were less used to courtrooms were more likely to be affected. Hence judges and courtroom officials were less likely to be aware of cameras than witnesses. However, the report notes the difficulty that respondents had in separating the stress of appearing before an international court and the presence of cameras:

> It was argued by many respondents that the nature of cross examination and the consequent pressure on a witness during a trial made testimony an exacting task. (Mason, 2000: 20)

Candid camera: other problems of cameras for the police

As we have already noted, the image management of the police is now an integral part of police–media relations. As well as the potential for cameras to affect the behaviour of officers in court, not least in adding to the strains of what is widely acknowledged to be a significantly stressful and unpopular aspect of police duties, there are also issues concerning the public perceptions of officers arising from courtroom footage and the uses to which this might subsequently be put. One of the very real potential problems for police officers giving evidence in a televised or recorded court case is the nature of the subsequent broadcast. Television by its very nature seeks to entertain as well as inform and as such, the practical realities of broadcasting court proceedings will inevitably mean the transmission of excerpts and highlights of the day's proceedings.

> People often form judgements based upon incomplete or inaccurate information. If viewers only see a selected part of a proceeding, such as a particularly entertaining portion of a witness's testimony or a lawyer's final argument and this is transformed into importance by repeated emphasis, the reality is distorted. When it is visualised, rather than verbally summarized it becomes an unalterable vision of truth. (Judge William L. Howard – South Carolina Bench, USA, in FOIA, 1996: 22)

It was precisely this fear that led the United States Judicial Conference in 1994 to end a three-year experiment with cameras in six federal state courts. This decision was taken despite the Federal Judicial Center concluding that no trial during the three years had been adversely affected. Several judges who sat on the Conference stated that they would reconsider their decision if proceedings were broadcast 'gavel to gavel', meaning in unexpurgated form.

Arguably it is what television does with the trial footage that could be most damaging to the police image. 'Playing vivid highlights of controversial trials rather than the pedestrian goings-on more representative of actual courtroom proceedings' (Hans and Dee, 1991: 137) could lead to police testimony being taken out of context. Altheide (1984) points out that this is due to the disparity in construction of judicial arguments and news stories. The story presented to judge and jury, he argues, is presented over the course of the trial: 'The parts are only meaningful in the context of the whole story' (Altheide, 1984: 298). In contrast, television news stories will focus on what is most interesting to the audience rather than what is necessarily most important to the proceedings. Reporters may use, for example, footage of an officer in an aggressive argument with defence counsel and join film with their own storyline. This could well create a narrative that may differ or depart from the central issue of the case. The image of an untrustworthy or unreliable police witness, for example, being 'caught out' on camera during cross-examination by an advocate over notebook entries (as in fact appeared to happen during an episode of *The Trial*), or perhaps seeming to prevaricate over the provenance of a tip-off from an informer, has the potential to cast wider aspersions on police probity and professionalism. Television, in its quest to please, will obligingly convert hours of legal argument and technicality into moments of compulsive viewing: 'Their tools will be imagination and analysis, distortion and dramatization, comment and comparison' (Goldfarb, 1995: 18). Added to this are the potential problems of re-presentations of court cases, where television seeks to edit the day's proceedings in order to entertain its audience. Such a process could lead to decontextualisation or worse still, re-contextualisation of police testimony into an entirely new narrative which bears only a passing resemblance to the day's proceedings in court.

A further interesting point concerns the 'coaching' of witnesses, already an issue that crops up in connection with payments, whether by the press or the police. As has already become something of a cliché in the US courtroom drama and in 'real' courtroom coverage on programmes such as *Court TV*, we may well see the Crown Prosecution Service, like their US District Attorney counterparts, being forced to respond on air to defence counsel's assertions that witnesses have been 'schooled' to give convincing evidence. Indeed, leading lawyers may discover that TV trial analysis in the manner of sports pundits is a lucrative sideline to professional practice.

Another possible effect that cameras in courtrooms might have is in terms of refocusing TV police drama. In considering police fiction, we have already noted how the cop show narrative tends to end at the point of capture and arrest. There are few if any court scenes in the police procedural, no sentencing and no prison. However, the increasing use of cameras in courtrooms may well heighten awareness of the court process and force the makers of police drama to include more courtroom scenes. If audiences become used to the drama of real-life court cases, it is highly likely that the producers of police drama will follow suit. A more unedifying prospect for the police, which follows directly on from our discussion of the rise of 'infotainment' programming in the previous chapter, is the possible emergence of courtroom blooper 'reality shows', in the style of the popular out-take *It'll be Alright on the Night/You've Been Framed* genre: the mental image of someone like Dennis Norden presenting excruciating evidence and testimonial trip-up clips in an offering called *Flops in the Box* may well not be too far removed from future reality. On a more serious note, in the context of re-examining testimony in alleged miscarriage of justice cases, it is just conceivable that future programmes in the tradition of *Rough Justice* may, as already occurs in reality TV shows like *Big Brother* and *The Experiment*, enlist the services of psychologists to analyse non-verbal communication in a search for evidence of deceptive behaviour in televised testimony. Against such a possible future backdrop, the title of the police training video *Officer Safety in the Witness Box* is surely a well-chosen one.

Chapter 9

Summing up

This book has attempted to provide an up-to-date overview of the changing dynamics and dimensions of the relationships that exist between the police and the media. We live in a world of instant reportage and endless entertainment, and continue to experience the growth of global cultural norms, tastes, moods and identities, phenomena that are inextricably linked with advances in new media, Internet technology and the pervasive international marketing of brand-name products and services. As Zalewski and Enloe put it a few years ago, 'We can drink Coke, eat sushi and watch *Neighbours* and be in practically any country in the world' (1995: 302). Though our primary focus has been on the British police–media nexus, as we have seen, it is increasingly difficult to isolate this from wider transnational trends. Indeed, to attempt such an uncoupling will in future become an ever more challenging and fruitless endeavour as the global media village environment continues to expand exponentially through the development of digital media, and reaches further into cyberspace with the extension of broadband Internet provisioning. But, the more things change, the more we would suggest that they also stay the same. Schlesinger and Tumber (1994: 6) noted that the public fascination with crime, offending, punishment and policing remain 'at the very heart of popular culture' and that, at least, shows no signs of abating. At the same time, there is, as Ian Loader (1997) has observed, an almost insatiable demand for policing services across a wide range of constituencies and media, including rapid developments in 'e-policing' services. That, too, we would suggest, is unlikely to diminish.

Factual, fictional and factional representations of policing in the media are the major – and for a great many citizens probably the sole – influence in shaping their perceptions and opinions about crime, law and order, community safety, police efficiency and integrity, not to mention the efficacy of criminal justice and penal policy. In a media democracy where information and immediacy are the drivers, soundbites, spin, sensation and celebrity have become core characteristics of media output across the ever-blurring boundaries between factual news, news-responsive drama, drama-documentary, dramatic reconstructions and reality TV. The tendency towards trivialisation and tabloidisation of news has been much lamented. The respected veteran foreign correspondent and parliamentarian Martin Bell (2002) has noted that in newsrooms nowadays, editorial judgement is often overridden by commercial calculation, while there are indications that journalism is itself becoming more of a 'performing art'.

At the same time, many fictional narratives about policing issues have arguably become more complex and challenging, bucking conventions, questioning stereotypes and engaging analytically with controversial aspects of crime and policing. In recent years, too, it has been the drama-documentary rather than the investigative journalistic exposé that has frequently been the more influential is tipping the scales of miscarried justice. In our 'synoptic society', the certainties of capture, arrest and police propriety once associated with the police procedural of some long-lost 'golden age' are now more likely to be found in the police 'reality' show, where uniforms are reassuringly resplendent, police driving and adherence to procedure impeccable, and the restoration of order is assured. The pixilated picture of the perpetrator of a car-crime caught on CCTV being bundled into the back of a police patrol car boasting a *Crimestoppers* logo is perhaps the embodiment of uncomplicated 'bite-sized' justice for the mass audiences of the *MTV* generation. Whereas for much of the latter half of the twentieth century, moral certainty has been the province of police fiction, nowadays such simplicity tends routinely to be located in the realm of infotainment. However, as we suggested in the previous chapter, that could, in the not too distant future, be overturned if there are further incursions into the courtroom setting through routine televising of proceedings.

The blurring of boundaries across the three domains of our title is also mirrored by the profile of an increasingly diverse 'cast of regulars' (to borrow a phrase from Loader and Mulcahy, 2001b), who have in various ways transcended traditional territorial divisions to mediate the public image and realities of policing. This cast of regulars contributes to the construction of a composite picture of policing which, of course, will vary across audiences, over time, according to social-demographic factors and in ways responsive to patterns of mass media consumption and preferences. We have noted the extent to which police organisations' own efforts in the management of their visibility have become more proactive and professionalised, the pre-packaging and strategic focusing of stories and storylines having become embedded as a mainstream activity rather than an optional extra. This extends far beyond the traditional press relations and PR functions associated with news management to include the provision of facilities, advice and briefings for the makers of films, documentaries and even soap operas, where 'authenticity' in representing and reproducing the 'realities' of policing and policework are regarded as valued and vital ingredients. The appointment of retired senior officers like John Alderson and Jackie Malton as specialist police advisers to fictional programmes is a well-established way of boosting the reality ratings of such enterprises. Awareness of the latest 'branded' crime crackdown operation in London, for example, is now as likely to enter the public consciousness via an episode of *The Bill* as through a spread in a Sunday supplement. The centrality of policing, both as a staple of media culture and its role as a much in demand 24-hour social service, is evident in the expanding inventory of 'experts', pundits and consultants who now speak about and for policing issues on the media across the three domains of fact, fiction and faction.

In addition to the spokespersons of individual constabularies and representatives of the various police staff associations, which of course have been added to in recent years by the voices of associations representing black, lesbian and gay officers, there are now many 'insider-outsiders' and 'outsider-insiders' from the ranks of retired police officers as well as academics and programme-makers who regularly appear in a variety of contexts to mediate the realities of policework. Among this postmodern patchwork of police–media 'experts' are individuals like John Stalker, former Deputy Chief Constable of Greater Manchester, who, having been at the centre of one of the greatest real-life policing dramas of the 1980s (recalled in his eponymous memoir of those events), is called upon regularly to comment on both real and reconstructed police investigations, while reassuringly endorsing awnings for the mature home-owner on daytime TV, in much the same way that actor Frank Windsor, who played the dependable Detective Sergeant Watt in *Z Cars*, does for financial services for the same audience. Nick Ross, the presenter of *Crimewatch*, has advised the Home Office on crime prevention and recently inaugurated the Jill Dando Institute for Crime Science at University College, London, in honour of his murdered colleague. The pioneering programme-maker Roger Graef, whose 1981 fly-on-the-wall documentary on the Thames Valley Police opened up for audiences the hidden realities of cop culture and policework, setting the standard for subsequent factual, fictional and reality police series, is these days 'Roger Graef the criminologist', equally at home at an academic police studies convention or commenting on police corruption on *Channel Four News*. Through his writings and his programmes, Graef has established himself over the last twenty years as one of the most faithful chroniclers of the realities of late-modern British policing, providing some timely reminders of the gaps that exist between fact, fiction and faction. As he wrote on revisiting Thames Valley in 2001:

> Between crime fiction and statistics we get a false idea of the grim treadmill that consumes most police effort. (Graef, 2001: 4)

That quote from Roger Graef leads us to another interesting question, namely the extent to which the police themselves may 'act up' or react to media constructions of policing. As Hurd noted:

> Historically, groups and institutions have always been concerned with the images of themselves produced by the media, and the police have been no exception to this concern. (1981: 54)

The fascination that real cops have with their fictional colleagues is apparent from the latter's involvement in real-life police social activities. *The Bill*, for example, used to have a golf team which did the rounds of provincial police forces, while a long line of TV police lead characters from Jack Warner to Tim Piggot-Smith has graced the top tables at official police functions, where they have been in much demand as after-dinner speakers, sometimes voicing views on 'real' policing and law and order issues to their appreciative hosts. From Barlow's bullying and Regan's violent vigilantism (Donald, 1985: 123–4), there have been recurring concerns about the extent to which fictional portrayals of policing, particularly those that emphasise the aggressive, action-centred machismo of police culture, may affect the behaviour of individual officers. In this regard there must surely be more than a suspicion that the 'capture culture' of *Blues and Twos* and high-speed car chases, glorified in countless media portrayals of police driving, may have played some part in the unacceptable risk-taking that resulted in the tragic 178 per cent increase in fatalities involving police pursuits recently reported by the Police Complaints Authority (PCA, 2002).

At the same time it is acknowledged that in acting as a kind of weathervane for the prevailing political mood, television may serve also to change, over time, police perceptions of particular styles, roles and specialisms within policing. For example, *Between the Lines* insiders believed that, against a backdrop of considerable debate inside the service about police ethics, their programme may actually have served to enhance the attractiveness and legitimacy of CIB work, a job much reviled in the heyday of *The Sweeney* when the 'rubber-heels' brigade of A10 were portrayed as yet another hurdle in the pursuit of villains and justice (Leishman, 1995). That real police respond to the images presented in TV fiction, was evident in a report concerning the actress Anna Carteret, who played Inspector Kate Longton in the 1980's drama *Juliet Bravo*. Ms Carteret, who was one of a number of demonstrators detained by the police during the May Day anti-globalisation demos in 2001, was apparently released after an officer recognised her as the famous fictional inspector (Logan, 2001). But perhaps the ultimate ironic example of boundary blurring resides in the fact that the winners of the first two British outings of the tropical island set reality show *Survivor* were both serving police officers.

In bringing our discussion to a close, we must return to the vexed and vexatious question of 'dominance or dependence' in the police–media relationship. While acknowledging the police's privileged position in terms of filtering facts and acting as information gatekeepers, we are in the end unpersuaded by conspiracy theories of a predominantly police-driven media agenda. The diversity and imperatives of the media industry in the end militate against the sustainability of such a position. Notwithstanding the justifiable concerns of journalists like David Rose (2001) that the police, in their dealings with the media, are only interested in 'what's in it for us?, that expression of negotiation works both ways. Among successful police public relations offensives, there are still to be found spectacular damage limitation failures. Though lazy reproductions of police press releases may abound, there are still incisive investigative exposés of police malpractice and incompetence. In the ecosystem of the information society, police and media work in symbiosis, constructing and reconstructing images of order that are perhaps more contingent than they used to be. We have faith in the intelligence of audiences to make up their own minds: we hope that this book will be of assistance in those deliberations.

References

Ainsworth, P. B. (1995) *Psychology and Policing in a Changing World*. Chichester: John Wiley.

Alderson, J. (1998) *Principled Policing*. Winchester: Waterside Press.

Allison, R. (2002) 'Child porn websites trigger 36 arrests', *The Guardian*, 21 May, p. 5.

Altheide, D. (1984) 'TV news and the social construction of justice: research issues and policy', in Surette, R. (ed.), *Justice and the Media: Issues and Research*. Springfield, IL: Charles C. Thomas.

Andersen, A. (1994) 'Reality TV and criminal justice', *The Humanist*, vol. 54, no. 5, pp. 8–14.

Audit Commission (1993) *Helping with Enquiries: Tackling Crime Effectively*. London: HMSO.

Baldwin, R. and Kinsey, R. (1982). *Police Powers and Politics*. London: Quartet Books.

Barak, G. (1994) 'Between the waves: mass mediated themes of crime and justice', *Social Justice*, vol. 21, no. 3, pp. 133–48.

Barber, S. (1983) 'The problem of prejudice: a new approach to assessing the impact of courtroom cameras', *Judicature*, vol. 66, no. 6, pp. 248–55.

Barker, M. (1997) 'The Newson Report: a case study in "common sense" ', in Barker, M. and Petley, J. (eds), *Ill Effects*, 1st edn. London: Routledge.

—— (1988) 'Television and the miners' strike', *Media, Culture and Society*, vol. 10, pp. 107–9.

Barker, M. and Petley, J. (2001) 'Introduction: from bad research to good – a guide for the perplexed', in Barker, M. and Petley, J. (eds), *Ill Effects*, 2nd edn. London: Routledge.

Barr, C. (1993) *Ealing Studios*, 2nd edn. London: Studio Vista.

Batchelor, S. (2001) 'The myth of girl gangs', *Criminal Justice Matters*, no. 43, pp. 26–7.

Bauman, Z. (1998) *Postmodernity and its Discontents*. Cambridge: Polity Press.

Beck, U. (1992) *Risk Society: Towards a New Modernity*. London: Sage.

Becker, S. and Stephens, M. (1994) 'Introduction: force is part of the service', in Stephens, M. and Becker, S. (eds), *Police Force, Police Service: Care and Control in Britain*. London: Macmillan.

Bell, M. (2002) 'Glamour is no good news', *Independent Tuesday Review*, 19 February, p. 8.

Berlins, M. (1997) 'Cheques and balances', *The Guardian*, 28 January, p. 17.

—— (2000) 'And can I say in my defence the law is simple: when a suspect is charged, newspapers must not publish anything that might prejudice a jury. And that includes campaigning for his or her defence. Are papers stepping over the line?', *The Evening Standard*, 18 October, p. 63.

Biafora, F. and Costello, R. (1999) 'Censoring the press: the Supreme Court rules on media ride-alongs', *Picturing Justice*, at www.usfca.edu/pj/censoring.

Bond, M. (1999) 'Stott's vice-like grip on stardom', *Sunday Times*, 10 January 1999.

Borgida, E., DeBono, K. and Buckman, L. (1990) 'Cameras in the courtroom: the effects of media coverage on witness testimony and juror perceptions', *Law And Human Behavior*, vol. 14, p. 489–509.

Bourdieu, P. (1998) *On Television and Journalism*. London: Pluto Press.

Boyle, R. (1999a) 'Spotlight Strathclyde: police and media strategies', *Corporate Communications*, vol. 4, no. 2, pp. 93–7.

—— (1999b) 'Spotlighting the police: changing UK police–media relations in the 1990s', *International Journal of the Sociology of Law*, vol. 27, pp. 229–50.

Brill, S. (1996) 'Cameras belong in the courtroom', *USA Today*, vol. 125, no. 2614, p. 52.

Brown, J. (2000) 'Occupational culture as a factor in the stress experiences of police officers', in Leishman, F., Loveday, B. and Savage, S. (eds), *Core Issues in Policing*, 2nd edn. Harlow: Pearson Education.

Brunsdon, C. (2000) 'The structure of anxiety: recent British crime drama', in Buscombe, E. (ed.), *British Television: A Reader*. Oxford: Oxford University Press.

Burgi, M. (1995) 'Case dismissed: networks maneuver to expand coverage of trials despite camera bans', *Mediaweek*, 13 November, vol. 5, no. 43, p. 16(1).

Butler, T. (2000) 'Managing the future: a chief constable's view', in Leishman, F., Loveday, B. and Savage, S. (eds), *Core Issues in Policing*, 2nd edn. Harlow: Pearson Education.

Button, M. (2002) *Private Policing*. Cullompton: Willan Publishing.

Caplan, J. (1989) *Televising the Courts: Report of a Working Party of the Public Affairs Committee of the General Council of the Bar*. London: HMSO.

Carey, S. (1993) 'Mass media violence and aggressive behaviour', *Criminal Justice Matters*, no. 11, Spring, pp. 8–9.

Cashmore, E. (1994) *... and there was television*. London: Routledge.

Chadee, D. (2001) 'Fear of crime and the media: from perceptions to reality', *Criminal Justice Matters*, no. 43, pp. 10–11.

Charman, S. and Savage, S.(1998) 'Singing from the same hymn sheet: the professionalisation of the association of chief police officers', *International Journal of Police Service and Management*, vol. 1, pp. 6–16.

Chibnall, S. (1977) *Law And Order News*. Tavistock: British Press.

Chiricos, T., Eschholz, S. and Gertz, M. (1997) 'Crime, news and fear of crime: toward an identification of audience effects', *Social Problems*, vol. 44, no. 3, pp. 342–76.

Clark, C. (1994) 'Courts and the media', *CQ Researcher*, vol. 4, no. 35, p. 817.

Clarke, A. (1983) 'Holding the blue lamp', *Crime and Social Justice*, vol. 19, pp. 44–50.

—— (1986) 'This is not the boy scouts', in Bennett, T. (ed.), *Popular Culture and Social Relations*. Milton Keynes: Open University Press.

Clarke, M. (1987) *Teaching Popular Television*. Crystal Lake, IL: Heinemann Educational Books.

Cohen, S. (1972) *Folk Devils and Moral Panics*. Harmondsworth: Penguin.

Corner, J. (2000) *Documentary in a Post-Documentary Culture? A Note on Forms and Their Function*, at www.lboro.ac.uk/research/changing.media.

Crandon, G. and Dunne, S. (1997) 'Symbois or vassalage?: the media and law enforcers', *Policing and Society*, vol. 8, no. 1, pp. 77–91.

Croall, H. (1998) *Crime and Society in Britain*. Harlow: Longman.

Cox, B., Shirley, J. and Short, M. (1977) *The Fall of Scotland Yard*. Harmondsworth: Penguin.

Denniston, L. (1994) 'Are federal cases headed for television?', *American Journalism Review*, vol. 16, no. 5, p. 50.

Ditton, J. and Duffy, J. (1983) 'Bias in the newspaper reporting of crime news', *British Journal of Criminology*, vol. 23, no. 2, pp. 159–65.

Dixon, T. L. and Linz, D. (2000) 'Overrepresentation and under-representation of African Americans and Latinos as lawbreakers on television news', *Journal of Communication*, vol. 50, no. 2, pp. 131–54.

Dominick, J. (1973) 'Crime and law enforcement in prime time television', *Public Opinion Quarterly*, vol. 32, pp. 241–9.

Donald, J. (1985) 'Anxious moments: *The Sweeney* in 1975', in Alvarado, M. and Stewart, J. (eds), *Made For Television: Euston Films Limited*. London: BFI.

Downes, D. and Morgan, R. (1997) 'Dumping the "hostages to fortune" ' in Maguire, M., Morgan, R. and Reiner, R. (eds), *The Oxford Handbook of Criminology*, 2nd edn. Oxford: Clarendon Press.

Dreyfuss, H. and Rabinow, P. (1982) *Michel Foucault: Beyond Structuralism and Hermeneutics*. London: Harvester Wheatsheaf.

Drummond, P. (1976) 'Structural and narrative constraints in *The Sweeney*', *Screen Education*, no. 20, pp. 15–36.

Duffy, J. (2002) 'Panic on the streets?', BBC Online, 21 February.

Dunkley, C. (1988) 'Fantasy, hypocrisy and verité viewed', *The Financial Times*, 20 April.

Dyer, C. (2002) 'Plan to make media payments to witnesses a criminal offence', *The Guardian*, 6 March, p. 1.

Dyer, R. (1993) *The Matter of Images: Essays on Representations*. London: Routledge.

Dykehouse, S. G. and Sigler, R. T. (2000) 'Use of the world wide web, hyperlinks and managing the news by criminal justice agencies', *Policing: an International Journal of Police Strategies and Management*, vol. 23, no. 3, pp. 318–38.

Eaton, M. (1995) 'A fair cop? viewing the effects of the canteen culture in *Prime Suspect* and *Between The Lines*', in Kidd-Hewitt, D. and Osborne, R. (eds), *Crime and the Media: the Post-modern Spectacle*. London: Pluto Press.

Edmund-Davies, Lord Justice (1979) *Committee of Inquiry on the Police*, Reports I and II, Cmnd. 7283 and 7633. London: HMSO.

Emsley, C. (1996) *The English Police: a Political and Social History*, 2nd edn. London: Longman.

Ericson, R. V. (1991) 'Mass media, crime, law and justice', *British Journal of Criminology*, vol. 13, no. 3, pp. 219–49.

—— (1994) 'The division of expert knowledge in policing and security', *British Journal of Sociology*, vol. 45, no. 2, pp. 149–75.

Ericson, R. V. and Haggerty, K. D. (1997) *Policing the Risk Society*. Oxford: Clarendon Press.

Ericson, R. V., Baranek, P. and Chan, J. (1987) *Visualising Deviance*. Milton Keynes: Open University Press.

—— (1991) *Representing Order*. Milton Keynes: Open University Press.

Evans, R. (1982) *The Fabrication of Virtue*. Cambridge: Cambridge University Press.

Fetveit, A. (1999) 'Reality TV in the digital era: a paradox in visual culture, *Media, Culture and Society*, vol. 21, pp. 787–894.

Fishman, J. (1999) 'The populace and the police: models of social control in reality-based crime television', *Critical Studies in Mass Communication*, vol. 16, pp. 268–88.

Fogg, E. (2000) 'Trident commander complains of advert "glamourising guns" ', *Police Review*, 8 September.

FOIA (1996) 'Cameras in the courtroom', *The Quill*, vol. 84, no. 8, p. 22.

Foucault, M. (1979) *Discipline and Punish: the Birth of the Prison*. Harmondsworth: Penguin.

Fowler, R. (1991) *Language in the News: Discourse and Ideology in the Press*. London: Routledge.

Fuller, M. (2001) 'Operation Trident targets London's rising gun crime', *Policing Today*, vol. 7, no. 2, pp. 22–5.

Fyfe, N. R. and McKay, H. (2000) 'Police protection of intimidated witnesses: a study of the Strathclyde police witness protection programme', *Policing and Society*, vol. 10, no. 3, pp. 277–99.

Gandy, O. (1989) 'The surveillance society: information technology and bureaucratic social control', *Journal of Communication*, vol. 39, no. 3.

Garfinkel, H. (1967) *Studies in Ethnomethodology*. Englewood Cliffs, NJ: Prentice-Hall.

Garland, D. (1990) *Punishment and Modern Society*. Oxford: Clarendon Press.

Garnett, T. (1999) at http://www.world-productions.com/wp/content/shows/cops/info/history.htm.

Garside, R. (2001) 'Putting the emotion back into crime: or how we can start to win the war of the headlines', *Criminal Justice Matters*, no. 43, Spring, pp. 32–3.

Gauntlett, D. (2001) 'The worrying influence of "media effects" studies', in Barker, M. and Petley, J. (eds), *Ill Effects*, 2nd edn. London: Routledge.

Gerbner, G. and Gross, L. (1976) 'Living with television: the violence profile', *Journal of Communication*, vol. 26, no. 2, pp. 173–99.

Gibson, J. (1999) 'Screen violence seen as fair play in right context', *The Guardian*, 11 May, p. 6.

Goldfarb, R. (1995) *TV or Not TV: Television, Justice and the Courts*. New York: New York University Press.

Gordon, C. (ed.) (1980) *Michel Foucault: Power/Knowledge*. London: Harvester Wheatsheaf.

Gordon, D. (1986) 'The electronic panopticon: a case study of the development of the national criminal records system', *Politics and Society*, vol. 15, pp. 483–511.

Graef, R. (2001) 'A policeman's lot is now a nastier one', *The Sunday Times*, 25 November, p. 2.

Graham, A. (1999) 'The cops talk shop', *Radio Times*, 9–15 October, pp. 20–2.

Green, P. (2000) 'American television: crime and the risk society', in Stenson, K. and Sullivan, R. (eds), *Crime, Risk and Justice*. Cullompton: Willan Publishing.

Greenslade, R. (2002) 'A storm in a chequebook', *The Guardian*, 11 March.

Greer, G. (2001) 'Watch with brother', *Review, The Observer*, 24 June, pp. 1–2.

Hagell, A. and Newburn, T. (1994) *Young Offenders and the Media: Viewing Habits and Preferences*. London: Policy Studies Institute.

—— (1997) 'Going public with young offenders and the media in Barker, M. and Petley, J. (eds), *Ill Effects*, 1st edn. London: Routledge.

Haggerty, K. D. and Ericson, R. V. (2000) 'The surveillant assemblage', in *British Journal of Sociology*, vol. 51, no. 4, pp. 605–22.

Haining, P. (1995) *On Duty With The Chief*. London: Boxtree Books.

Hall, S., Critcher, C., Jefferson, T., Clarke, J. and Roberts, B. (1978) *Policing the Crisis: Mugging, the State and Law and Order*. London: Macmillan.

Hamilton, A. (1998) 'Can TV be trusted with real life? Extract from the Huw Weldon lecture to the royal television society', in *The Independent*, 14 October, p. 4.

Hans, V. and Dee, J. (1991) 'Media coverage of law', *Behavioural Scientist*, vol. 35, no. 2, p. 135.

Harrington, V. and Mayhew, P. (2001) *Mobile Phone Theft*, Home Office Research Study 235. London: HMSO.

Heath, L. and Gilbert, K. (1996) 'Mass media and fear of crime', *American Behavioral Scientist*, vol, 39, no. 4, pp. 378–92.

Hernandez, G. (1996) 'Courtroom cameras debated', *Editor and Publisher*, vol. 129, no. 7, p. 24.

Hicks, J. and Allen, G. (1999) *A Century of Change: Trends in UK Statistics Since 1900*. London: HMSO.

Higham, N. (2002) 'Witness payments under scrutiny', BBC Online, 5 February.

Hill, A. (2000) 'Crime and crisis: British reality TV in action', in Buscombe, E. (ed.), *British Television: a Reader*. Oxford: Oxford University Press.

Hogan, D. and Mason, P. (1999) 'Let the people see the Lockerbie trial', *The Times*, 9 February, p. 21.

Hoggart, M. (1998) 'We're all voyeurs now', *Vision, The Times*, 10 January, p. 2.

Hoggart, P. (2000) 'The old bill soldiers on', *The Times*, 7 July.

Holdaway, S. (1983) *Inside The British Police*. Oxford: Basil Blackwell.

Holland, P. (1996) 'Conscience of the age?', *The Times*, 6 November, pp. 23–4.

Home Office (1993) *Inquiry into Police Responsibility and Rewards* (Sheehy Report). London: HMSO.

Hope, Lord Justice (1994) 'Television in the Scottish Courts', unpublished paper from Meeting of Chief Justices and Attorneys-General of the European Union (Lisbon), House of Commons Library Research Paper 99/111.

Howard, K. (2001) 'Is it a crime to seek refuge?', *Criminal Justice Matters*, no. 43, pp. 32–3.

Howitt, D. (1998) *Crime, the Media and the Law*. Chichester: Wiley.

Huff, J. (2000) *The Southall Rail Accident Inquiry Report*. London: Health and Safety Executive.

Hunt, A. (1997) 'Moral panic and moral language in the media', *British Journal of Sociology*, vol. 48, no. 4, pp. 629–48.

Hurd, G. (1976) '*The Sweeney* – contradiction and coherence', *Screen Education*, no. 20, pp. 47–53.

—— (1981)'The television presentation of the police', in Bennett, T. (ed.), *Popular Television and Film: a Reader*. London: BFI.

Innes, M. (1999) 'The media as an investigative resource in police murder enquiries', *British Journal of Criminology*, vol. 39, no. 2, pp. 269–86.

—— (2000) ' "Professionalising" the role of the police informant: the British experience', *Policing and Society*, vol. 9, no. 4, 357–83.

Jaffe, J. (1991) *New York State Bar Memorandum*. New York: NYSBA.

Jefferson, T. and Hollway, W. (2000) 'The role of anxiety in fear of crime', in Hope, T. and Sparks, R. (eds), *Crime, Risk and Insecurity*. London: Routledge.

Jempson, M. (2001) 'Blood on the news-stands', *Criminal Justice Matters*, no. 43, pp. 24–5.

Jenkins, C. (2000) 'Pressing the point', *Policing Today*, vol. 6, no. 1, pp. 23–5.

Jenkins, J. (1993) 'Convicted by Fleet Street' *Criminal Justice Matters*, no. 11, p. 3.

Johnson, M. (1993) *Electronic Media Coverage of Courtroom Proceedings: An Evaluation of the Pilot Program in Six District Courts and Two Courts of Appeal, Report of the Federal Judicial Conference of the United States*, 4 November.

Johnston, L. (1992) *The Rebirth of Private Policing*. London: Routledge.

—— (1998) 'Street crime in England and Wales', in McKenzie, I. (ed.), *Law, Power and Justice in England and Wales*. London: Praeger.

—— (2000) *Policing Britain: Risk, Security and Governance*. Harlow: Longman.

Kassin, S. (1984) 'TV cameras, public self-consciousness and mock jury performance', *Journal of Experimental Social Psychology*, vol. 20, pp. 336–49.

Kennedy, I. (2001) *Learning from Bristol: The Department of Health's Response to the Report of the Public Inquiry into Children's Heart Surgery at the Bristol Royal Infirmary 1984–1995*, Cm 5363. London: HMSO.

Kershaw, C. *et al.* (2001) *The 2001 British Crime Survey: First Results, England and Wales.* London: Home Office.

Kilborn, R. (1994) 'How real can you get? Recent developments in reality television', *European Journal of Communication*, vol. 9, pp. 421–39.

Kilborn, R. and Izod, J. (1997) *An Introduction to Television Documentary: Confronting Reality.* Manchester: Manchester University Press.

Kinsey, R., Lea, J. and Young, J. (1986) *Losing the Fight Against Crime.* Oxford: Blackwell.

Laing, S. (1991) 'Banging in some reality: the original "Z Cars" ', Corner, J. (ed.), *Popular Television in Britain: Studies in Cultural History.* London: British Film Institute.

Lassiter, C. (1996) 'TV or not TV – that is the question', *Journal of Criminal Law and Criminology*, vol. 86, no. 3, pp. 928–1095.

Lees, S. (1995) 'Media reporting of rape: the 1993 British "date rape" controversy', in Kidd-Hewitt, D. and Osborne, R. (eds), *Crime and the Media: The Post-Modern Spectacle.* London: Pluto.

Leighton, P., Woods, P. and Berry, R. (2001) 'Easy access and more choice @ northumbria.police.uk', *Policing Today*, vol. 7, no. 2, pp. 14–17.

Leishman, F. (1995) 'On screen – police on TV', *Policing*, vol. 11, no. 2, pp. 143–52.

Leishman, F. and Savage, S. P. (1993) 'The police service' in Farnham, D. and Horton, S. (eds), *Managing the New Public Services.* London: Macmillan.

Levi, M. (2001) 'White-collar crime in the news', *Criminal Justice Matters*, no. 43, pp. 24–5.

Loader, I. (1997) 'Policing and the social: questions of symbolic power', *British Journal of Sociology*, vol. 48, no. 1, pp. 1–18.

Loader, I. and Mulcahy, A. (2001a) 'The power of legitimate naming: Part I – chief constables as social commentators in post-war England' *British Journal of Criminology*, vol. 41, no. 1, pp. 41–55.

—— (2001b) 'The power of legitimate naming: Part II – making sense of the elite police voice', *British Journal of Criminology*, vol. 41, no. 3, pp. 252–65.

Logan, B. (2001) 'Bravo, Juliet', *The Guardian*, 9 May 2001, G2, p. 4.

Lord Chancellor's Department (2002) *Payments to Witnesses: a Proposed Criminal Offence of Making, or Agreeing to Make, or Receiving Payments to Witnesses in Criminal Proceedings.* London: HMSO.

Luft, G. (1997) 'Stopping the circus: "dignified" coverage of the Oklahoma City case', *Columbia Journalism Review*, March–April, vol. 35, no. 6, p. 11.

—— (1993) 'An electronic Panopticon? A sociological critique of surveillance theory', *Sociological Review*, vol. 41, pp. 653–78.

Lyon, D. (1993) *The Electronic Eye: the Rise of Surveillance Society.* Cambridge: Polity Press.

Lyon, D. (2001) *Surveillance Society: Monitoring Everyday Life.* Buckingham: Open University Press.

McLaughlin, E. and Murji, K. (1998) 'Resistance through representation: "storylines", advertising and police federation campaigns', *Policing and Society*, vol. 8, no. 4, pp. 367–400.

Macpherson, Sir W. (1999) *The Stephen Lawrence Inquiry: report of an Inquiry*, Cmnd Paper No. 4262-i. London: HMSO.

Manning, P. (1997) *Police Work*, 2nd edn. Prospect Heights, IL: Waveland Press.

Mark, R. (1977) *Policing a Perplexed Society*. London: Allen & Unwin.

Mason, P. (1992) *Reading the Bill: an Analysis of the Thames Television Police Drama*. Bristol: Bristol Centre for Criminal Justice.

—— (2000) *The Impact of Electronic Media Coverage of Court Proceedings at the International Criminal Tribunal for the former Yugoslavia*. The Hague/ Southampton: ICTY/Centre for Media and Justice.

Mathiesen, T. (1997) 'The viewer society: Michel Foucault's "panopticon" revisited', *Theoretical Criminology*, vol. 1, no. 2, pp. 215–33.

Mauro, T. (1994) 'Why are cameras still banned in federal courts?', *The Quill*, vol. 82, no. 2, p.12.

Mawby, R. C. (1997a) 'Cops on the box', *Policing Today*, vol. 3, no. 1, pp. 32–5.

—— (1997b) 'Making sense of media representations of British policing: implications for the police image', *Security Journal*, vol. 9, pp. 139–42.

—— (1998a) 'Policing the image', *Criminal Justice Matters*, no. 32, pp. 26–7.

—— (1998b) 'The changing image of policing in television drama 1956–1996', *Journal of the Police History Society*, pp. 39–44.

—— (1999) 'Visibility, transparency and police–media relations', *Policing and Society*, vol. 9, no. 3, pp. 263–86.

—— (2001) 'Promoting the police? The rise of police image work', *Criminal Justice Matters*, no. 43, pp. 44–5.

—— (2002) *Policing Image: policing communication and legitimacy in modern Britain*. Cullompton: Willan Publishing.

Mawby, R. I. (2000) 'Core policing: the seductive myth', in Leishman, F., Loveday, B. and Savage, S. P. (eds), *Core Issues in Policing*. Harlow: Pearson Education.

Maxfield, M. (1984) *Fear of Crime in England and Wales*. London: HMSO.

—— (1987) *Explaining Fear of Crime: Evidence from the 1984 British Crime Survey*. London: HMSO.

Morgan, D. (1998) 'Showbusiness', *Policing Today*, vol. 4, no. 3, pp. 46–7.

Morgan, R. and Newburn, T. (1997) *The Future of Policing*. Oxford: Oxford University Press.

Mulley, K. (2001) 'Victimised by the media', *Criminal Justice Matters*, no. 43, pp. 30–1.

Mulraney, S. (2001a) 'Telling it straight', *Police Review*, 13 July 2001, pp. 26–7.

—— (2001b) 'Targeting fear', *Police Review*, 26 October, pp. 20–1.

Murdock, G. (1982) 'Disorderly images: television presentation of crime and policing', in Sumner, C. (ed.), *Crime, Justice and the Mass Media*. Cambridge: Institute of Criminology.

—— (2001) 'Reservoirs of dogma: an archaeology of popular anxieties', in Barker, M. and Petley, J. (eds), *Ill Effects*, 2nd edn. London: Routledge.

Murji, K. (1998) *Policing Drugs*. Aldershot: Ashgate.

Nellis, M. and Hayle, C. (1982) *The Prison Film*. London: Radical Alternatives To Prison.

Neville, E. (2000) 'The public's right to know – the individual's right to privacy', *Policing and Society*, vol. 9, no. 4, pp. 413–28.

New York State Committee to Review Audio-Visual Coverage of Court Proceedings (1997). *An Open Courtroom: Cameras in New York Courts*.

Newburn, T. (1999) 'To serve and collect', *Criminal Justice Matters*, no. 36, pp. 11–12.

Neyroud, P. (1999) 'Danger signals', *Policing Today*, vol. 5, no. 2, pp. 10–15.

Neyroud, P. and Beckley, A. (2001) *Policing, Ethics and Human Rights*. Cullompton: Willan Publishing.

Norris, C. and Armstrong, G. (1999) *The Maximum Surveillance Society: the Rise of CCTV*. Oxford: Berg.

Norris, C. and Dunnighan, C. (2000) 'Subterranean blues: conflict as an unintended consequence of the police use of informers', *Policing and Society*, vol. 9, no. 4, 385–412.

Oliver, M. (1994) 'Portrayals of crime, race and aggression in "reality based" police shows: a content analysis', *Journal of Broadcasting and Electronic Media*, vol. 38, no. 2, pp. 179–92.

O'Shaughnessy, M. (1999) *Media and Society: an Introduction*. Oxford: Oxford University Press.

Parker, J. (1986) 'The organizational environment of the motion picture sector', in Ball-Rokeach, S. and Cantor, M. (eds), *Media, Audience and Social Structure*, Beverly Hills, CA: Sage.

Pearson, G. (1983) *Hooligan: A History of Respectable Fears*, London: Macmillan.

Pengelly, R. (1999) '*Crimewatch*: a voyeurs paradise or public service?', *Police Magazine*, January at www.polfed.org/magazine/01_1999/01_1999_voyeurs.htm.

Pike, L. (1968) *The History of Crime in England*. London: Patterson Smith.

Pines, J. (1995) 'Black cops and black villains in film and TV crime fiction' in Kidd-Hewitt, D. and Osborne, R. (eds), *Crime and the Media: the Post-Modern Spectacle*. London: Pluto Press.

Police Complaints Authority (2002) *Annual Report of the Independent Police Complaints Authority*. London: PCA.

Poniewozik, J. (2000) 'Fighting inner demons: the makers of *Homicide* aim to arrest viewers' attention with a very personal police series', *Time*, vol. 155, no. 12. p. 99.

Poster, M. (1997) *The Second Media Age*. Cambridge: Polity Press.

Povey, D. and Rundle, S. (2001) *Police Service Strength*, Home Office Statistical Bulletin 23/01. London: HMSO.

Punch, M. (1979) 'The secret social service', in Holdaway, S. (ed.), *The British Police*. London: Edward Arnold.

Rawlings, P. (2002) *Policing: a Short History*. Cullompton: Willan Publishing.

Reiner, R. (1978) 'The new blue films', *New Society*, vol. 30, pp. 706–8.

—— (1981) 'Keystone to *Kojak*: the Hollywood cop', in Davies, P. and Neve, B.

(eds), *Politics, Society and Cinema in America*. Manchester: Manchester University Press.

—— (1989) 'The politics of police research', in Weatheritt, M. (ed.), *Police Research*. Aldershot: Avebury.

—— (1994) 'The dialectics of Dixon: the changing image of the TV cop' in Stephens, M. and Becker, S. (eds), *Police Force, Police Service*. London: Macmillan. pp. 11–32.

—— (1997) 'Media made criminality', in Maguire, M., Morgan, R. and Reiner, R. (eds), *The Oxford Handbook of Criminology*, 2nd edn. Oxford: Oxford University Press.

—— (2000a) 'Romantic realism: policing and the media', in Leishman, F., Loveday, B. and Savage, S. P. (eds), *Core Issues in Policing*, 2nd edn. Harlow: Longman.

—— (2000b) *The Politics of the Police* 3rd edn. Oxford: Oxford University Press.

—— (2001) 'The rise of virtual vigilantism: crime reporting since World War II', *Criminal Justice Matters*, no. 43, Spring, pp. 4–5.

Reiner, R., Livingstone, S. and Allen, J. (2000a) 'Casino culture: media and crime in a winner–loser society', in Stenson, K. and Sullivan, R. (eds), *Crime, Risk and Justice*. Cullompton: Willan Publishing.

—— (2000b) 'No more happy endings? The media and popular concern about crime since the Second World War' in Hope T. and Sparks, R. (eds), *Crime, Risk and Insecurity*. London: Routledge.

Reith, M. (1999) 'Viewing of crime drama and authoritarian aggression: an investigation of the relationship between crime viewing, fear and aggression', *Journal of Broadcasting and Electronic Media*, vol. 43, no. 2, pp. 211–24.

Richards, P. (1999) *Homicide Statistics*, House of Commons Library Research Paper 99/56.

Robards, B. (1985) 'The police show', in Rose, B. (ed.) *T.V. Genres: a Handbook and Reference Guide*. Westport, CT: Greenwood Press.

Roberts, M. (2001) 'Just noise? Newspaper crime reporting and the fear of crime, *Criminal Justice Matters*, no. 43, pp. 12–13.

Roffman, P. and Purdy, J. (1981) *The Hollywood Social Problem Film*. Bloomington, IN: Indiana University Press.

Rose, D. (2001) ' "What's in it for us?" ', *Criminal Justice Matters*, no. 43, pp. 8–9.

Roshier, R. (1973) 'The selection of crime news by the press', in Cohen, S. and Young, J. (eds), *The Manufacture of News*. London: Constable.

Ross, N. and Cook, S. (1987) *Crimewatch UK*. London: Hodder & Stoughton.

Rushdie, S. (2001) 'Who will rehabilitate the British tabloid press?', *The Guardian Saturday Review*, 7 July, p. 12.

Sacco, V. (1995) 'Media constructions of crime', *Annals*, no. 539, pp. 141–54.

Savage, S. P. and Leishman, F. (1996) 'Managing the police: a force for change?', in Farnham, D. and Horton, S. (eds), *Managing The New Public Services*, 2nd edn. London: Macmillan.

Schlesinger, P. and Tumber, H. (1993) 'Fighting the war against crime – television, police and audience', *British Journal of Criminology*, vol. 33, no. 1, pp. 19-32.

—— (1994) *Reporting Crime: the Media Politics of Criminal Justice*. Oxford: Clarendon Press.

Schramm, W., Lyle, J. and Parker, E. B. (1961) *Television in the Lives of Our Children*. Stanford, CA: Stanford University Press.

Shapland, J. and Vagg, J. (1987) 'Using the police' *British Journal of Criminology*, vol. 27, no. 1, pp. 54–63.

Shipman Inquiry (2001) *Independent Public Inquiry into the Issues Arising from the Case of Harold Frederick Shipman*, at www.the-shipman-inquiry.org.uk.

Short, E. (1981) 'Evaluation of California's experiment with extended media coverage of courts', cited in Stepniak, D. (1998).

Slapper, G. and Tombs, S. (1999) *Corporate Crime*. Harlow: Longman.

Soothill, K. and Walby, S. (1991) *Sex Crime in the News*. London: Routledge.

Sparks, A. B. and Staszak, D. D. (2000) 'Fine tuning your news briefing', *FBI Law Enforcement Bulletin*, vol. 69, no. 12, p. 22.

Sparks, C. (1988) 'Striking results?', *Media, Culture and Society*, vol. 10, pp. 369–77.

Sparks, R. (1989) 'Dramatic power; television images of crime and law enforcement', in Sumner, C. (ed.), *Censure, Politics and Criminal Justice*. Milton Keynes: Open University Press.

—— (1992) *Television and the Drama of Crime: Moral Tales and the Place of Crime in Public Life*. Milton Keynes: Open University Press.

—— (2001a) ' "Bringin' it all back home": populism, media coverage and the dynamics of locality and globality in the politics of crime control', in Stenson, K. and Sullivan, R. (eds), *Crime, Risk and Justice*. Cullompton: Willan Publishing.

—— (2001b) 'The media, populism, public opinion and crime', *Criminal Justice Matters*, no. 43, pp. 6–7.

Stanko, E. A. (2000) 'Victims R Us: the life history of "fear of crime" and the politicisation of violence', in Hope, T. and Sparks, R. (eds), *Crime Risk and Insecurity*. London: Routledge.

State of Arizona (1980) *Information Service Memorandum IS 88.002, TV Cameras in Court, Evaluation of Experiments*.

State of Nevada (1980) *Final Statistical Report Cameras in the Courtroom in Nevada*.

State of New Jersey (1994) *Electronic Media Coverage of Courtroom Proceedings: Effects on Witnesses and Jurors, Supplement Report of the Federal Judicial Centre to the Judicial Conference Committee on Court Administration and Case Management*.

Stenson, K. and Croall, H. (2001) 'Editorial', *Criminal Justice Matters*, no. 43, p. 3.

Stephens, M. and Becker, S. (eds) (1994) *Police Force, Police Service: Care and Control in Britain*. London: Macmillan.

Stepniak, D. (1998) *Electronic Media Coverage of Courts – Report for the Federal Court of Australia*.

Stepp, C. (1998) 'The fallout from too much crime coverage', *American Journalism Review*, vol. 20, no. 3, p. 55.

Stockdale, J. and Gresham, P. (1995) *The Presentation of Police Evidence in Court*, Home Office Police Department Police Research Series Paper No. 15. London: HMSO.

Tombs, S. and Whyte, D. (2001) 'Reporting corporate crime out of existence', *Criminal Justice Matters*, no. 43, pp. 22 3.

Travis, A. (1999) 'Police chief: this can't go on', *The Guardian*, 19 February.

Trigobov, D. (1997) 'Court coverage hindered by OJ backlash? Simpson debacle has changed the landscape for cameras in courtrooms', *Broadcast and Cable*, vol. 127, no. 26, p. 24.

Tulloch, J. (1990) *Television Drama: Agency, Audience and Myth*. London: Routledge.

Vance, J. L. (1997) 'Media interviews: a systematic approach for success', *FBI Law Enforcement Bulletin*, vol. 66, no. 2, pp. 1–8.

Vine, I. (1997) 'The dangerous psycho-logic of media "effects" ' in Barker, M. and Petley, J. (eds), *Ill Effects: the Media Violence Debate*. London: Routledge.

Waddington, P. A. J. (1991) *The Strong Arm of the Law*. Oxford: Oxford University Press.

Wakeham, Lord (1999) 'Justice must always come first', *News of the World*, 5 December, p. 8.

Walker, J. (ed.) (1997) *Halliwell's Film Guide*. London: HarperCollins.

Walklate, S. (2000) 'Equal opportunities and the future of policing' in Leishman, F., Loveday, B. and Savage, S. P. (eds), *Core Issues in Policing*, 2nd edn. Harlow: Longman.

Wall, D. (2001) 'Cybercrimes and criminal justice', *Criminal Justice Matters*, no. 46, pp. 36–7.

Waters, I. (2000) 'Quality and performance monitoring' in Leishman, F., Loveday, B. and Savage, S. P. (eds), *Core Issues in Policing*, 2nd edn. Harlow: Longman.

Webster, C. (2001) 'Representing race and crime', *Criminal Justice Matters*, no. 43, pp. 16–17.

Welch, M., Fenwick, N. and Roberts, M. (1997), 'Primary definitions of crime and moral panic: a content analysis of experts' quotes in feature newspaper articles on crime', *Journal of Research in Crime and Delinquency*, vol. 34, no. 4, pp. 474–94.

Welsh, T. and Greenwood, W. (2001) *McNae's Essential Law for Journalists*. London: Butterworths.

West, W. (1997) 'Television in court invites trivialization', *Insight on the News*, vol. 23, no. 23, p. 48.

White, R. and Perrone, S. (1997) *Crime and Social Control*. Oxford: Oxford University Press.

Williams, P. and Dickinson, J. (1993) 'Fear of crime: read all about it?' *British Journal of Criminology*, vol. 33, no. 1, pp. 33–56.

Wilson, C. (1995) 'Legal fears over live crime show', *The Sunday Telegraph*, 8 October, p. 4.

Wilson, J. Q. and Kelling, G. L. (1982) 'Broken windows: the police and neighbourhood safety', *The Atlantic Monthly*, March, pp. 29–38.

Winston, B. (1990) 'On counting the wrong things', in Alvarado, M. and Thompson, J. (eds), *The Media Reader*. London: BFI.

Wintour, P. (2000) 'TV series stoke fear of crime', *The Guardian*, 7 November, p. 8.

Wykes, M. (2001) *News, Crime and Culture*. London: Pluto Press.

Wynn-Jones, R. (1997) 'Victim "mugged" again by TV crime show', *The Independent*, 4 May, p. 6.

Young, J. (1971) *The Drug Takers*. London: Paladin.

—— (1997) 'Left realist criminology' in Maguire M., Morgan, R. and Reiner, R. (eds) *The Oxford Handbook of Criminology*, 2nd edn. Oxford: Oxford University Press.

Zalewski, M. and Enloe, C. (1995) 'Questions of identity in international relations', in Booth, K. and Smith, S. (eds), *International Relations Theory Today*. Cambridge: Polity Press.

Index